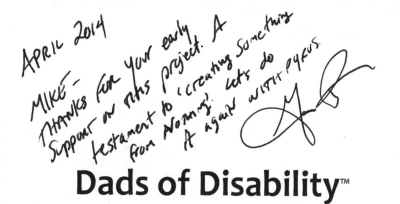

APRIL 2014

MIKé —
THANKS for your early
support on this project. A
testament to "creating something
from Nothing". Let's do
it again with pqfus.

Dads of Disability™

Stories for, by, and about fathers of children who
experience disability (and the women who love
them)

Collected, edited, and some written by Gary Dietz
Additional editing by Beth Gallob
Poetry selected by Marly Youmans
Foreword by MaryAnn Campion

Published by Gary M. Dietz
Brookline, New Hampshire, US
www.dadsofdisability.com

Dads of Disability

Published by Gary M Dietz, PO Box 21, Brookline, NH 03033 USA
www.dadsofdisability.com

ISBN: 0615971865
ISBN-13: 978-0615971865

http://www.dadsofdisability.com
gdietz@garydietz.com

 Find us on Facebook   Like us at
www.facebook.com/dadsofdisability

 @garymdietz
#dadsofdis

March 2014 edition 1.0

For Alexander

Dads of Disability

Contents

Admiration

Transformation

Transition

Coda

Dads of Disability

Foreword

When I first joined the ranks of the genetic counseling profession, I knew that I would have the pleasure of meeting hundreds of extraordinary individuals along the way. The families that come through our doors include children with rare disabilities and diagnoses who find the strength and resiliency to accomplish more than the world expected.

Simultaneously, their parents discover an ever-growing capacity for love, acceptance, patience, and discernment. To say the least, these mothers and fathers are charting unknown territory on a daily basis, with little more than gumption and good instincts to guide the way. Over the past few decades, the volume and variety of resources available to assist these families has grown immensely due to the tremendous efforts of advocacy groups. However, many individuals in the disability community continue to feel alone—isolated from the world they once knew and immensely lonely for someone else who understands.

Unfortunately, most of the support literature that exists today has been developed for and by women: moms, sisters, daughters, and grandmothers, all trying to lend a hand, an ear, or a shoulder to another mother or family in need. Meanwhile, resources for, by, and about fathers have been few and far between, with limited places for men to turn when they find themselves facing life's unexpected challenges. To make matters worse, men are often less inclined to seek counseling and support, which only exacerbates the negative feelings that may already be present—feelings of frustration, incompetence, fear, anxiety, or worse. Not a moment too soon, *Dads of Disability* has the potential to empower fathers to see their position through a different lens—one of hope, self-respect, and companionship.

What's more, parenting resources often focus solely on the rosy, cheerful stories that are meant to inspire promise and perseverance. While those stories are incredibly important (some of which are included in this book!), it is equally important for parents to know that they can speak the truth, no matter how raw, exhausted, painful, and even *selfish* it might sound. Those are the stories that give other parents the real courage to keep going, knowing that they aren't the only ones who have had those thoughts and that they haven't been deserted.

In an era of political correctness, many writers are afraid to tell their stories about disability unless the language is perfectly acceptable to all parties. And yet, aiming for that level of acceptance is probably a fruitless endeavor and a disservice to the community. Wouldn't we rather have authors who speak authentically, paying more credence to their message than their terminology? (Terminology that may change even before the next edition of this book appears!) After all, they are the only ones who are actually living through the experience. In that regard, I applaud Gary Dietz and the other contributors for telling it like it is, honestly and without apology.

Dads of Disability is also incredibly timely. Cultural shifts in the United States and many other countries have led to increased paternal involvement in childrearing. However, acceptance of these altered responsibilities has come much more slowly, meaning that men today often encounter a complex web of judgment, pity, and admiration in their caregiver role, particularly when you factor in a disability. This book provides a context for fathers to hear accounts from various stops along the voyage, each one a reminder that mothers and fathers share many of the same experiences, but their vantage points may be drastically different. Different isn't better or worse; it is merely an alternative perspective.

Parenting a child of any age with special needs unearths an array of obstacles, regardless of the child's specific diagnosis. Some disabilities are isolated, while others are multi-systemic; some are congenital, while others are acquired; some worsen, some plateau, and some resolve. And some are terminal. Despite which categories describe your loved one, the practical and emotional odysseys depicted in this book will likely seem familiar and comforting to all. Again, the most salient and palpable message emphasizes universality and understanding.

For over a decade, I've had the joy of teaching and supervising genetic counseling master's students who are soaking in as much knowledge as possible in their two short years of graduate school. I continually remind them that they will learn more from families than from the world's greatest textbook or lecture. Undoubtedly, hearing stories from the main stage of life carries a level of accessibility that enables details and themes to be remembered for eternity. We also stress the importance of truly seeing each person without the veil of their diagnosis or disability.

The essays and poems included in this book will allow you to see not only the children but also the parents with a clarity that defies expectations. You may choose to read bits and pieces over time or devour the book in one sitting, depending on the needs and demands of your own here and now. Regardless of your course, you will feel more solid and connected simply for having taken the journey.

MaryAnn Campion
Boston, Massachusetts, January 2014

Ms. Campion is the founding director of the Master of Science Program in Genetic Counseling at the Boston University School of Medicine.

Introduction

Welcome to my book!

Why have I put so much passion into this project? What things made me afraid about it? And how did I overcome my fears? Plus, so many people to thank for making this project come to fruition.

Why this collection?

Let me explain why this collection exists and what it is and isn't supposed to be. I hope you'll read this volume with these thoughts in mind.

In my journey as a father, I reached out for many kinds of support. But the books, articles, online support groups, and websites I encountered were almost always written or moderated by or specifically for women or families. And while the quantity and quality of online support for men as parents of children with disabilities has started to improve (there are some great father's blogs), extensive content for and by men *generally* remains lacking.

The central theme of the pieces in this collection is around fathers. Yet, the book *does not* exist to diminish or ignore any other constituency. Not mothers, not women in general, not children (young or adult), nor anyone in the disability community at large.

In a situation that recurred a few times during the creation of this book, some reviewers told me, "Great story, but I want to learn more about what the child went through!" I actually agree. I would like to learn more about the child, too. More details of the child's story would indeed be compelling. However, the focus of the pieces in this *specific collection* is on the father's experiences and emotions. The supporting details of the child and extended family are there to move the father's narrative or the narrative about the father forward. This is purposeful and not disrespectful to other players.

If you are looking for stories that provide more detail about the child in the story, or the mother, or the extended care team, or pieces written by disabled folks themselves, or about larger societal issues and advocacy, there are many other wonderful books to explore. I continue to. You should, too.

My fears and skepticism

I was afraid of many things as I planned and began this project. I was afraid that nobody would care. I was afraid that folks of any gender would think that men had no right to write about this topic and should just "quit their whining and man up." (Fear not, there is no "whining" in this book.) I was afraid that I could convince no women to publicly write about their spouses or co-parents. I was afraid that the stories would seem overly preachy, overly saccharine, or worst of all, not interesting. I was afraid of getting criticism from disabled youths and adults themselves as well as activists saying that I published something intentionally hurtful. Or willfully ignored certain folks. Or not helpful. Or selfish.

Fears and skepticism put to rest!

Here is what I learned about my fears during this project. I learned that there was a pent-up demand for everyday dads of disability to tell stories from a variety of perspectives. That many fathers feared that their stories were unique, when, in fact, they were fairly common. I learned that women from many backgrounds and experiences rely on, appreciate, and admire the fathers of their children in many different ways—and were willing to talk about them publicly in great detail. I learned (actually, I was reminded) that what we observe in Studs Terkel's books is true: Everyone has a story. You just have to ask them.

After explanation, most people understand the genesis of this project and why and how it exists and have been incredibly supportive.

But I re-learned that you can't make all people happy all the time, and you can't make some people happy ever. For example, there are "people first" language users who want you to write, "a person with autism" rather than an "autistic person." And there are some people who demand it be written the other way to empower autistic people. I acknowledge that the title "Dads of Disability" itself is a term that is not "people first." But the book's subtitle does use a people first phrase when it says "children who experience disability." I try to use both people first and non-people first language in this collection, but I also needed to keep the individual author's language usage in place as much as possible.

I have taken a deep breath, examined my ethos and the feelings in my heart, and remind myself that you can offer some people free puppies and candy, yet there will always be a few who say "how dare you offend the allergic and diabetic!"

Authentic human stories offered with love and open arms

I offer this collection with as much love and authenticity as I can. I offer it with open arms to those who are receptive to reading and to those who may not be. I ask only that readers be open to embracing the emotional lives, experiences, and opinions of the fathers and mothers and children who have shared their thoughts about themselves, their families, and the dads of disability in their lives. And if there is unintentional offense, please let it *start* or *continue* a dialog, not *end* one.

It is my sincere desire that these essays and poems will foster discussions with your loved ones and your community. Please enjoy them.

With warm regards,

Gary Dietz
Brookline, New Hampshire, US
March 2014

Beginnings

We're all fathers. But we're all different.

Most dads of disabilities start—or continue—their experiences as fathers in the same way that fathers of typically developing children do. In innumerable, unique ways.

Sometimes the reality of a disability hits a dad hard. Sometimes it is subtle. Sometimes we feel nothing for a long, long time. And then it hits us all at once, later and more intensely than one would expect.

There is no "right" way to begin the journey of being a father of a child with a disability.

Dads of Disability

1

26 Days

In the first 26 days of my son's life, I did more for him than my father has done for me in my entire life.

Like far too many African Americans, I grew up without a father in my home, and I have yet to meet him. So when my wife became pregnant, I was excited to be a different, better kind of father. Once we were informed that the child would be a boy, my wife immediately said, "We need to name him Damian Jr. after his daddy." This child was to be a legacy builder.

Everything leading up to the delivery was perfect. We had no idea of what was about to take place. We arrived at the hospital with the highest hopes of meeting this little guy, the one who we had been talking to, praying for, and bonding with. In the delivery room, we watched the nursing staff grow increasingly anxious as they quickly entered and exited.

We were told that they had to get Damian Jr. out quickly as his oxygen level was dropping. By the time I was in the surgery room, my wife was already cut open, and they were pulling our son out. He was blue, and that is hard for a black kid! I watched, slack jawed, as they resuscitated him. This lasted about a minute, but it seemed like hours. My son opened his eyes as they rolled him passed us, but it would be some time before we would see his eyes again.

The next morning we discovered the harsh reality. Damian Jr. had a global brain injury and was not given much hope for survival. As a pastor, I am supposed to have words for moments like this. The truth is that I had nothing but tears and prayers.

My wife just had major surgery, so it was time for me to step up. For the first few days, I was the one at Damian's side. For newborns, skin-to-skin contact is necessary, so it was Damian Jr. and daddy. I would sing and pray and rock my son, who had tubes and sensors connected all over his little body. His father was his everything.

I found myself having to be his defender as some doctors were pretty much giving up on him. They assumed that we blindly believed something that would never happen. As people of faith, we understood what they were telling us, we just didn't agree about the outcome. Indeed, it was time to become a defender of my family.

Most hospitals focus on the mother as the main person with whom to communicate. Because my wife was recovering, I made the medical staff call me. I wanted to know everything that was happening. If Damian Jr. made any improvements or setbacks, I would be the first to know. I was the first line of defense—his first line of defense.

The doctors said, "He will probably never breathe on his own." That same night, I received a call saying he coughed out his respirator. They said, "He will probably never open his eyes." And they said, "He will never cry." But within 24 hours he would prove them all wrong.

I realized that I couldn't determine what progress he would make, but I could hope for the best and pray that God would perform a miracle. And that is exactly what we saw, day by day. We never gave up on our son, and he kept fighting.

Cerebral palsy, seizure disorder, developmental delay, and so many more diagnoses would be in our future. While those early days made me a father, they also made a man out of me. Although my own fatherlessness has left more scars than I can count, I was determined my son would not feel that pain.

Times still get hard, but I remember the lessons I learned in those first 26 days of Damian's life, and I continue to fight for my family. That is what a husband, a father, and a man does!

- *Damian Boyd*

Dads of Disability

2

The Second Time Around

Zeke is our young child from my second marriage to a great woman named Theresa.

They are my second family. I have other children who are well into adulthood. Theresa and I got together later in life, and she's somewhat younger than I am. It was always her dream to have children, and she was very up front with me at the beginning about that. I told her that kids didn't scare me. Little did I know that I would soon be scared by things I never imagined I would have to deal with.

So we started a family. Theresa was pregnant with our first child, and one week before her due date, the baby died in utero. We grieved, but we didn't give up. She was starting to approach the age where the pundits say it gets more difficult to have a successful pregnancy. To us, the situation almost became frantic.

We were finally blessed with our son Zeke. And like many of the stories that you hear in what would become our situation, the first nine months of his life were pretty much on target. He was developing typically. Then at one year of age Zeke started to regress.

Theresa noticed it first. She was pretty sure there was something going on with Zeke at about 15 months. We talked to the pediatricians, but they didn't seem alarmed. In one incident when Zeke was about six months old where Theresa was *sure* he was having seizures, we went in they said, "Oh no; they all do that." You can probably hear the tone yourself right now: "Oh, no, that's pretty normal."

Theresa persisted, and we finally enlisted the help of the local community services agency. Sure enough we get over to the hospital, and Zeke is diagnosed with autism. While they do more testing and don't find anything, we're pretty sure there's something else going on.

At least Theresa was. I was pretty much in denial. I said what you could imagine an older guy like me could say. "He's just a kid; you know there's nothing wrong with him. He's fine." My denial came from a combination of my cultural background, the experiences I had with my now-adult children from my previous marriage, and that general promise from the professionals that 99 times out of 100 nothing is wrong.

All kids are different, and certainly in my previous experience anything strange that the child went through always resolved. Every child develops at his or her own pace. Even I had every childhood disease that's on that list at the bottom of the medical form, except polio. Mumps, measles, chicken pox, rheumatic fever, scarlet fever; I had them all. And I was fine. I always said that kids are over-doctored today. Leave them alone; let them grow up.

And boy was I wrong. I am so thankful that Theresa was hyper-vigilant, while I was still in the "ah he's a kid; you know he's going to be okay" stage.

One night my wife was completely exhausted, and she went to sleep. I mean, we hadn't slept more than three or four hours at a time in four years. For some reason, I woke up in the middle of the night, and Zeke was not in his room. I went downstairs, and he was in the bathtub with his pajamas on in ice cold water.

That was pretty much the moment that I realized that I needed to pay much closer attention to what was going on with my son. The cold water shocked us both. I finally told myself that *the second time around wasn't going to be anything like I experienced with my older children.*

Theresa remained adamant that there was something else going on. She didn't need to convince me anymore, so we went to Hanover, New Hampshire, the location of Children's Hospital at Dartmouth (CHAD), where Zeke had some tests done. Everything came back pretty normal except that Zeke did have sleep apnea.

Zeke got a tonsillectomy and adenoidectomy. They brought him out, and when he woke up, he was just absolutely wild with pain and ripped his IV out. They hadn't given him any pain medication.

Here's this little kid who can't talk. (He also has apraxia.) And there are four or five doctors and nurses and me trying to hold him down, so they can put the IV back in. By the time they had tried six times, I was almost screaming. My face was 10 inches away from the doctor and I said, "You have one more chance, and if you don't get it in, you're going to give him a fucking injection. Do you understand me?" I think he just totally ignored me because the nurse got it in on the next try.

Zeke has always had gut issues, which is very common with autistic kids. So we had him on a casein and gluten-free diet. There was a nutritionist in the hospital, and we told her, "No, he can't eat this. No, he can't eat that." Then she stood at the little station right outside the room and in a very loud voice said, "Can you spell 'nutrition'?" in about as condescending a tone as anyone could ever use. Like we didn't know how to take care of our child. Like we were doing something detrimental.

We made a request for food that was on his diet, and his first breakfast showed up. The kid has just had a tonsillectomy and adenoidectomy, and they sent English muffins and dry cereal. Now who feeds that to a kid whose throat is raw? And who is on a gluten-free diet? What were they thinking?

The saga continued, and we persisted because we knew that something was wrong. Sometime when you make a comment about an issue to a doctor that isn't quite on the ball, the doctor says, "Oh, well he's autistic" as if that is a rational answer to a complex issue you are bringing up. I don't want to bash doctors because many of them are fantastic. It's just that they don't always know the answers and often won't tell you that they aren't sure. And in my experience, more often than not, many tend to discount the knowledge that parents bring to bear about their child.

Finally, we saw another doctor at CHAD, a pediatric neurologist who had quite a bit of experience with autism. He said, "I want to do 24-hour EEG." Sure enough, Zeke was having seizures about every ten minutes. His seizures are in the left temporal lobe which controls speech. This is also why he doesn't sleep. The seizures wake him up.

So after all of the previous testing, when they said, "No, there is no brain damage, and no, he's not having seizures, and no, there isn't anything wrong" he actually *was* having seizures, and there *was* something medically wrong.

Then the neurologist ordered a lead screening test, even though Zeke had already been tested when he was two. We happen to live in an old farmhouse, and sure enough, Zeke's got lead toxicity.

We also saw a gastroenterologist about Zeke's chronic diarrhea, and we found a probable cause of Zeke's uncontrollable fits and biting. He had an impacted colon.

There can be many kinds of unintended consequences caused by the lack of humility in the so-called expert's observation and communication with families. For example, Zeke's a climber. A year ago, he fell and broke his hip, and those treating him automatically assumed that he had been abused. They got him in the operating room, got all his clothes off, and saw that he didn't have a mark or a bruise on him.

Here's another example of where listening to the experts doesn't always match the reality of your child. My dad passed away last December. The summer before, he was in Mass General Hospital. We went down to visit, and Zeke saw my dad in the hospital bed, all hooked up to IVs and tubes.

While some so-called experts will tell you that autistic kids aren't supposed to have much emotion or compassion, the very first thing that Zeke did was crawl into bed with my dad and give him a big hug. He knew exactly where his grandfather was and that there was something wrong with him. I'm not sure he has the concept of "grandfather" yet. But because Zeke knew and loved him, crawling into the hospital bed was his way of showing that he understood.

I'm forever in debt to Theresa for teaching me that just because I had done this before didn't mean that my experiences would be the same this time around. I guess the doctors need to be more like Theresa, or at least listen to folks like her, and learn the same lessons she taught me.

I made a conscious decision to have a second family later in life. We had a plan that went awry when we discovered Zeke's challenges. I learned to listen to Theresa, who simply saw what was right in front of her. Over time, I was able to face my current reality. Just because the first time around was easy didn't mean I wouldn't have a whole lot more to handle the second time around.

- Nate Weiner

3

Men at Work

More money. More responsibility. Less travel. This new job was going to be *fantastic*.

I had a great first few days with my new manager. My research showed this company was going to have a bright future. And I was hired in a role where I would have some access to the executive team and make a *real* impact. During my first two weeks, I was invited for a 2-on-1 meeting with both the CEO and the VP of sales! Yes, this was going to be a great career change.

Both of the executives I was meeting with were male and more or less 20 years older than I was. I walked in as they were chatting (bragging, really) about the many accomplishments of their children. What schools, what clubs, what grades, what new jobs. It was the usual form that family small-talk banter takes in the workplace on steroids. This conversation seemed to be a bit fueled by alpha-male bravado.

I was there for at least five minutes listening intently to them regaling stories of their children. I suspected I would soon learn that one of them was well on the way to curing cancer or creating a perpetual motion machine. All of a sudden, the CEO turned to me and said, "I hear you have a baby. Tell us about him!"

Bringing me into the conversation. My chance to be "one of the boys." Sure, no problem.

But then I tried to speak ... Nothing.

It's not like I have a problem talking off-the-cuff. But nothing was happening. Nothing external anyway. Inside my head, it was a completely different story.

My son, who had exhibited numerous challenges since birth, received his genetic diagnosis a few short weeks before I started this new job and sat in on this meeting. So, this very conversation was probably the first time I was hearing a father, older than I and having already achieved a level career success I thought I wanted to emulate, actually talking about his children. And it sort of sent me into a mini state of shock.

During what was really probably only five seconds, every single negative scenario my brain could muster up flashed in my minds eye: disease, intellectual challenges, physical problems, serious behavioral issues, operations, institutional care, special schools. You name it, and it flashed before me. Rational or not. Probable or not.

And then I slowly started to cry.

That was *not* what these two executives were expecting to see. And it was *not* what I was expecting to happen.

Well, these two executive dads were certainly nice to me. As I recall, they said the standard supportive things and let me know that whatever I needed, I should just ask. And I honestly don't doubt that they meant what they said.

But they didn't pay much attention to me again during my tenure at that firm. Perhaps it was the quality of my work. Perhaps it wasn't anything I did or said at all. Perhaps it was the unexpected emotion shown on our first meeting. But even though there were other issues, I felt that my tenure at that company was doomed because I acted human and not particularly "manly" during a time I was supposed to punch my ticket to enter the executive club.

I always wonder how that meeting would have gone if I had cried in front of two female executives? Would it have been the same experience? Better or worse? Would the female execs have thought I was condescending to them and treating them as "mother" rather than boss? (For that matter, did the male executives feel I was treating them as "father" rather than boss?) Or would it have made me seem more human to the female execs and thus would have made my tenure with them easier? I'll never know for sure. But what I *do* know is that those two men I was scheduled to bond with in a business sense never spoke to me on a personal level again. And our professional interactions ended up being very rare.

Now, don't get the idea that I am a blubbering fool whenever something challenging comes up. I only experienced that level of semi-public emotion again one more time during the next dozen or so years (see the essay *Smartphone Tears* in this volume). People cry for different reasons and in different contexts, and it is all okay. But I did learn a lot from that experience in that conference room. My main takeaways are easy to summarize but profound in impact.

First of all, I learned that I must always try to be compassionate with everyone at work. Who knows why a person is having a bad day? Was it a bad night of sleep, or did she just have a horrible fight with her husband? Was it a just a cold coming on, or is his father moving into a memory care facility? Did this person at work just get a difficult diagnosis about their child and believe that nobody else in the world, much less at work, had ever felt such pain? I learned to try to show interest in others' stories. And if those stories are really hard, to make the time to listen to the pain, their issues, and be human. Even if it is at work.

The next thing that I learned is that even strong people can be weak sometimes. And that can make them even stronger. In the years since that office cry, I've really watched how the public and private people I intensely admire are really just plain-old people. That's why I like biographies so much, I guess. Seeing people whose "public-relations face" is all power and strength and finding out that the man or woman behind the curtain is, for the most part, just like the rest of us.

Finally, most directly, after sharing the story of the office cry with others, I found out that this incident is not unique. I am not the only person that this has happened to! One person in particular, a few years my senior, in his version of the "office cry" meeting told me of a completely parallel situation where he revealed to the executives that his son had just died weeks before.

Many years after the "office cry," I was working for another company and attending an out-of-state trip to their annual sales conference. I got a mobile call from one of my son's helpers. I was told that after more than a year of working with a therapy horse, my son finally got up and rode on it! On a saddle! I was overjoyed. I had to share this news immediately with someone who would "get it."

A male executive in this company, not much older than I was, had a child with a severe disability. I asked him to come aside with me to an empty buffet room in the conference center next to our main meeting. I leaned my head in and started to put my arm around him. He was a bit taken aback, but indeed he was quite a different executive from the ones I mentioned from earlier in my career. I started to smile and laugh. And yes, cry some tears of joy. I told him why I felt as I did, what my son had just done, that I was so happy, and that I thought he would understand. He smiled, patted me on the back, and said he was happy for us and glad I could trust him to share and understand the importance of this personal news. I was kind of embarrassed and told him I wasn't looking for a father figure, just someone who would really "get" the good news I just received.

I grabbed a napkin off of a table, cleaned up, and then after a firm handshake, we walked back to the main area of the sales conference. Most importantly, I worked successfully at that company and with that executive for a number of years after this event with no impact on my career from our interaction.

- Gary Dietz

You can see an animated vignette of this story as a part of the Dads of Disability video at:

http://blog.dadsofdisability.com/animation

Dads of Disability

4

Letter To My Son

How could we know at first
that anything was wrong? You were
the only baby we had cared for.
When you cried for hours at a time
and couldn't stop, despite
our efforts to appease, to feed,
rock, bathe, and change,
we thought that this must simply
be the way of babies, the part
that no one mentioned in the books.

And after all, you were
so perfect, dark eyes fringed
as a flower, starfish hand
splayed in my palm, but as you grew,
"terrible two" went on for years.
You wouldn't eat, seldom slept,
bending nature to your will.
At first, the doctors found no problem.
Sometimes I wondered if we might
just be imagining, hoped it was so.
I would watch you race around
the house, your face almost

a double of my own at four or five,
superhero cape streaming behind
a paradigm of movement.
Sometimes I'd hold you upside down
just to still you for a moment,
and we'd both laugh and laugh
at that vain gesture. Sometimes
your rage would suddenly surprise me

when a favorite game had to end
or the bath had grown too cold
or my energy would ebb.
Where did a child that small
gather all that strength?
Teachers and doctors tried
to give this thing a name,
to make you fit; you grew
angrier instead. Yet wild apples
mellow on the branch and so did you.

Now grown, you're well equipped
to grapple with the world. I wouldn't
have you other than you are.
Let your will bend others always
toward the good. What seems to be
infirmity can prove a gift.

- *Robbi Nester*

5

The Girl with the Trauma Tattoo

While getting her ready for bed, our then 3-year-old daughter, Ava, had an epic meltdown. It was her singular masterpiece—her Mona Lisa—the kind of unraveling that makes you seriously reconsider if you're even fit to be a parent. It nearly drained the life out of us. Sheer physical exhaustion was the only reason my wife and I were able to sleep that night.

Nevertheless, we awoke the following morning strangely reinvigorated by the idea that it was a new day, a new chance for Ava to react in appropriate ways to life's simplicities.

The first thing she did that morning was flip out because her younger sister put the step stool away before she could. To be clear, if "flip out" has a literal meaning, that is what I am describing here. I am not using hyperbole. What I mean is that she had to be physically (and safely, don't worry) restrained from doing harm to herself and others and that it lasted a very long time and lingered because she can neither soothe herself nor be soothed.

When I dropped her off at school that morning, I had to peel her off of me like a wailing amoeba. "NO DADDY! NOOOOOOO!" As if out of some dramatic movie scene, I had to close the door as she reached for me in vain while several teachers held her back. As I walked down the hallway to leave, a mom who was bearing witness to the chaos looked at me and said, "Don't you just wish you knew when days like this were coming?"

I responded with a restrained grunt and a mild half-smile, "I know when I wake up it's going to be a day like this."

I then expected a normal parent-to-parent response to that, something like, "Tell me about it!" Instead she responded with a seemingly judgmental, "Really?"

Well, yeah. Really.

She had no idea.

I stewed as I walked to my car. Was this woman questioning my methods, like I'm to blame for a daughter who struggles daily with behaviors? Does she think I'm one of those dads—the kind who are too preoccupied, distant, or laid back to enact discipline? The kind who enable such dramatic public behavior thanks to a laissez-faire attitude at home?

Au contraire, mon frère. I am Discipline Dad! I always follow through and never make empty threats. I dole out timeouts like business cards. I will leave a restaurant as the food arrives to sit in the car with Ava if she's giving us attitude. Shoot—I will make her sit there and watch other kids enjoying cake at a birthday party if she misbehaves. I don't play around. How dare this woman equate me with one of those dads. I am the dad who is freestyle parenting those dads' kids at the playground: "Hey, kid—give the young lady a turn on the slide and get that finger out of your nose, will ya?"

I mean, I am Discipline Dad, right? After all, my own father instilled in me a healthy fear of him and authority in general. I can still hear the sound of his fast-paced, stomping footsteps coming up the stairs following the melodramatic cries of my younger sister as a result of something I may or may not have done. I was taught to have manners and show respect, and a glare from across the room was all it took to set me straight. I have raised my daughters in the same loving way. Or at least tried to.

This woman just... well, she had no idea.

§

My wife and I became licensed foster parents in 2008. As an in-home speech and language therapist, she works with many foster families and eventually felt the call. Upon getting to know some of the kids and families she works with, I was sold as well.

Our hope was to eventually adopt through foster care (fost-to-adopt), a hope that swelled as it became increasingly apparent we'd be unable to have children of our own. (Thanks a lot, sperm.) While originally filling out the fost-to-adopt paperwork, we were asked to describe our "ideal" child, an exercise that helps the agency match families and kids.

After seeing several foster placements come and go, we were blessed with a three-month-old baby girl who somehow perfectly matched our description. We adopted Ava in June of 2010.

When we tell people Ava is adopted, I'm pretty sure most imagine the musical play, movie, and soundtrack of my life, "Annie." I can hear their internal, sing-song monologue say, "Awww! How sweet. Happily ever after."

Indeed, I am extremely happy, and I love our daughters beyond words. (We adopted Ava's younger sister in the summer of 2013, also through foster care). But my goodness, no. "Annie" is not our scenario. The movie ends with Annie joyously riding an elephant at a backyard carnival. (Although Ava enjoys calling me Daddy Warbucks while playing pretend, I have yet to be able to afford a pet elephant or even to rent one.) But our movie would end with Annie going out of her mind so hard she passes out because Daddy Warbucks had the audacity to tell her to dismount the elephant for bedtime. Then she awakens to punch the elephant in the face and walks away in slow motion as things explode in a fireball behind her.

Adoption from foster care is not exactly like the movies.

Ava was abandoned at the hospital after nine months of a drug and possibly alcohol-infused pregnancy. She was born addicted to, among other things, methamphetamine and spent her first three days of life in detox. She went from the hospital to a foster home to another foster home before landing with us. She did not have a name.

We knew adopting a drug-exposed child out of foster care could present issues and behaviors. Ava presents symptoms for disorders as mild as ADHD (I'll take it!) and as severe as schizophrenia (no thanks!). And those are just two future possibilities. To date, Ava has actually been diagnosed with two other disorders.

Ava has reactive attachment disorder. It is a serious clinical condition whereby a neglected or abused child has extreme difficulty developing healthy bonds with parents or caregivers. It's called RAD but it is definitely not rad. Its hallmarks are defiance and difficulty being comforted, which are also Ava's hallmarks. That's hallmarks not

Hallmark, although they should make Hallmark cards for this:

Sorry about your kid's RAD... (open card)
...Maybe it will get better? (picture of rainbow)

Ava also has sensory integration disorder. My wife and I went to a training class on SID, and they passed out a sheet of symptoms and said, "Check whichever ones you feel like your child struggles with." I was like CHECK, CHECKITY-CHECK, CHECK. CHECK YOURSELF BEFORE YOU WRECK YOURSELF. DOUBLE-CHECK. INFINITY CHECK.

There are different levels of SID, but Ava has the kind where she seeks and absolutely needs sensory input at all times. This means running, jumping, crashing into things, purposely banging her head on the wall, throwing herself on the ground in a heap of despair, doing somersaults on rocks, walking over hot coals—things like that. When she is 10 years old, she is totally going to approach us and say that she wants to drop out of school and join the circus so she can be shot out of a canon every day. I will say, "You're not hangin' with carnies!"

SID is actually kind of cool for me as a dad because I often find myself not knowing what to do. My go-to parenting move is throwing Ava up in the air or tackling her for no reason, which apparently helps—a lot. Her therapists say, "That's great! Keep giving her that proprioceptive input." Indeed, that was my plan all along. My wife is always saying, "Stop throwing her so high, she's gonna hit her head on the fan!" and I say, "Chill out, babe, I'm trying to do this propro-septic reboot."

Oh yeah, the therapists. There are several. Really.

§

My wife's background as a therapist enabled her to notice things very early on with Ava that many might have missed. As a result, our daughter currently has three therapists.

Her physical therapist (PT) has done wonders with the four-month old we handed her who could not hold her head up. Not including illegal narcotics, Ava did not receive any pre-natal care, which caused her to have the physical strength and stamina of banana pudding. Now she is more athletic than many kids her age, and last year won a "long jumping contest" at school. On those days when she's being particularly difficult around other well-behaved children and their parents, I walk away thinking smugly, don't judge us—she can jump farther than all of you!

Ava also receives occupational therapy (OT), where she works on the fine motor skills needed for everyday life and gets to do physical things that stimulate her brain activity. At first I thought occupational therapy was going to find her a job, although that unfortunately has not happened—yet. Her PT and OT, who have seen her since she was a baby, are God-sent angels from heaven who have taught Ava how to walk, run, swim, and live, and who have the patience of ten Mother Teresas. It's like, who taught YOUR kid how to walk? YOU? Pfft.

Finally, she has straight-up behavioral therapy. That's right—Ava sees a child psychologist. (Did I mention she is three?) Once a week she's looking at flashcards of blurry images and telling her therapist they look like the monsters that scare her in the night.

That was not a tasteless joke—Ava has night terrors. I'm sure it has nothing to do with spending nine months in a meth womb. She doesn't even know where she is or who she is when she "wakes up" from these episodes. She's completely out of it and, as always, cannot be soothed.

This trauma during sleep has caused Ava to have an extreme anxiety about sleep. So it wasn't a surprise to us when she started exhibiting behaviors during nap time at school. After meetings with school administrators (fun!), we had to eliminate nap time altogether, which helped but also means she is spent by the end of the day. This leads to its own brand of behaviors, making it impossible to tell if they're the result of her being tired, her traditionally-defiant age, or her specific developmental issues.

It's cool when, after a long day at work, you pick up your kids and you try to leave school except your no-napping daughter randomly decides to go bonkers in the hallway because the Velcro strap on her shoe came loose. "Hey, why not just re-strap it?" you say calmly but through clenched teeth. Except everything just gets worse. Now she is rolling around on the floor, and everyone is looking, and before you know it you are flying high on a metaphorical cloud of confused rage. That is called: WEDNESDAY.

This scene, the scene in the school administrator's office, or the scene where I'm leaving the playground carrying a hysterical child like a football, is not the scene I envisioned when I imagined myself a father.

I imagined myself as Discipline Dad, rarely, if ever, having to endure such embarrassment. I imagined myself like my dad.

Although I am naturally calmer than my (Italian, Brooklyn-born) wife, it's always supposed to mean more when dad swoops in. You got dad mad? Uh-oh, watch out! But Ava rarely watches out, and my attempts at discipline are met only with more defiance and zero humility. Nothing has stuck, and I'm rendered unable to diffuse a public meltdown save for removing her entirely.

My dad glare doesn't work.

§

Ava is beautiful, sweet, smart, funny, active, warm, and extremely outgoing. You could meet her, as many have, and find her to be no different than the average child. Even our extended family often has a difficult time believing that our nurture did not easily overcome her nature. But Ava wears her trauma like a hidden tattoo, and you need to look really hard—or, you know, live with her—to see that it's there.

Even for us there is a temptation to say, to believe, she's been with us essentially her entire life, and she doesn't remember being abandoned. She was just a baby! Everything is fine now. So why isn't she heeding our demands?

The truth is this: Ava was abandoned and she knows it. No matter how horrific her nine months in utero, or how traumatic her first days on Earth, she was abandoned. That familiar voice, no matter how loud, silent, or profane, was gone the very instant she entered this world. She'll never get over it. Our job is to help her cope.

Fear of abandonment takes on many forms, but the form most closely associated with me losing my mind once and for all is Ava's absolute need for control.

She is on a never-ending quest for control of her environment because she does not yet fully trust that we, her parents, will always be there. Surrendering her will to ours makes her feel very unsafe and extremely vulnerable. This means everything from going absolutely insane because I handed her the blue toothbrush when she wanted the green one to sabotaging every possible good thing we provide her by demanding more. Ava never wants anything—be it a treat, TV show, time at the pool, people visiting, whatever—to end because it means her surrender to forces (usually us) beyond her control. In her subconscious mind, the last time she surrendered she was left all alone in a cold hospital room. She'll be darned if she let's that happen again.

You wanted to cry a little bit there, right? Me, too. But guess what? When you're in the throes of one of these episodes, and it's the fifth one that morning, it's pretty difficult to draw upon that reality. It's pretty difficult to supplant discipline with sensitivity. Where is the line?

The line, I have come to learn, is probably somewhere in between me gently closing the door and blowing her a kiss as her teachers carry her away, and the feeling of anger I get when I perceive that someone else thinks I'm the issue.

It's somewhere in between a five-minute hug and a five-minute timeout.

It's allowing her to color in church instead of forcing her to sit and listen because you know she can't do that. Even though you promised yourself years ago that church would be a no-coloring zone.

It's understanding that she cannot be parented like you were because never for a second did you fear your parents would not always be there. (And also because your mom wasn't addicted to meth. Right, Mom?)

It's putting aside your egotistic wish to be viewed as a dad who demands the utmost respect in exchange for catering to her needs.

Of course, my frequent inability to discern this line has often made me feel like an unworthy, inconsistent dad, forever trying and failing at new ways to handle everything. Which makes me oh so different than—no parent, ever.

I need to get over it. So, hopefully, she can.

I need to stop worrying about how I'm perceived by others and do my job. Besides, I am Discipline Dad. I just, you know, occasionally work alongside my sidekick, Captain Sensitivity. Together we battle our arch nemesis RAD and his minions, other parents with "The Look."

Sure, Ava can be a handful to put it mildly, but few have any idea where she's come from and besides, we got this, okay—so back off. She is going to make it, gosh darn it, and so are we. She's overcome so much already and will continue to do so.

Because one day, the girl with the trauma tattoo will jump farther than anyone ever thought she could.

- *Mike Kenny*

6

Coffee, Tea, or God?

A few years ago when my son was smaller and experienced fewer outbursts of a lesser impact, we ventured cross country to the Pacific Northwest to visit friends. It was just him and me. He of boundless energy, occasional explosive outbursts, and supreme cuteness. Me, the sole adult responsible for us both for a week. My sleep saved up (I was going to get hardly any that week), a strategic packing of toys, snacks, pull-ups, and an artistically duct-taped and bungied kid cart (it's kind of giant stroller/wheelchair). This wasn't going to be easy. But I was going to give the boy as close to a typical holiday week as any other family could expect.

We miraculously made it through security and boarding and takeoff. Smooth flying!

Of course, sooner or later, there would be a mid-flight bathroom break, something I faced with trepidation. After I had walked Alexander to the lavatory in the back of the plane; convinced attendant #1 to hold a blanket in front of the partially open lavatory door for his privacy; gotten his leg braces and pants down, assisted him in going, cleaning up, and getting redressed; washed our hands;

wiped down his leg braces with disinfectant cloths; wiped off the lavatory seat (he didn't make it dirty, but I'd be damned if the next occupant would think that my child made the lavatory dirty, so I left it cleaner than when we got there); gotten him back to his seat; wiped the sheen of sweat off my forehead; taken a very deep breath; and hoped that he would play with his twiddle toy long enough so that I could go take a pee myself.

After all of this, I ventured back to the lavatory myself. I asked to cut to the front of the line, and folks graciously let me. (I find it so hard that parents of typical developing kids get so resentful of the line cutting thing. It isn't just a nice-to-have. It's often a necessity.)

I turned on my super hearing. I needed to hear if there was anything happening back at our seats through a lavatory door and airplane noise. And I engaged "super-peeing speed," something that a man at my age was beginning to be hard pressed to engage. Never does a man so regret the onset of an aging prostate as when he needs to relieve himself quickly so as to ensure his son doesn't freak out on an airplane.

After the quickest urination my body would allow and skipping hand washing (I had wipes in my pockets I'd use later), I exited the lavatory. Over the seat tops, I saw my son happily playing with his twiddle toy and looking out the window. I took advantage of this reprieve to take a cleansing breath and use a hand wipe across my hands and forehead.

I felt a tap on my back and turned around to see attendant #2, the partner of the one who had draped our earlier open-door bathroom experience. She had a smart modern haircut, a motherly smile, and was probably about

20 years older than I. In a relaxed but regionally-unspecific southern accent, she asked, "What's your boy's name?"

"Alexander."

"He's a doll. You know, God chose you to be his dad. You are doing a great job."

OK. Deep breath.

Do I just say thanks, and go back to my seat? Do I get into a theological discussion with a stranger? I'm supposed to be a patient man. A good man. An open-minded liberal of the traditional small "l" variety. But we had just been through security. Through checking in a heavy mobility device after waiting in a long line. Through getting a decent set of seats. Through who-knows-what bacteria on my son's leg braces. Through 400 calories burned and a shirt sweated through just to get two people to be able to pee. Was this really a time for this conversation?

Support groups say it isn't my responsibility to engage the public—unless I want to.

But my son was happily in his seat for who knows how long and not pinching anyone. Since I could see his cute head and he was happily playing, I decided to engage with attendant #2.

"Thanks, but although I usually believe in a God, I am not sure that God specifically recruited me for Alexander."

"Oh, sure He did. God only gives people what they can handle."

Another deep breath.

"Well, what about the half-dozen dads of kids with disabilities I know who are crappy dads? The ones that run away. The impatient ones. The abusive ones. Did God choose them to be crappy dads? Or did I make the conscious decision to be a good dad, and God happened to be fully behind my good choices?"

"Well, God has His ways. And you are a good man." Indeed, a nice compliment. But how exactly could she know I was a "good man?"

Yet another deep breath. This one was just to stop me from sweating so profusely, but she probably heard it as exasperation. "Thanks so much. I appreciate your kind words. But I'd like to own my own successes and failures as not necessarily predestined. Sorry if I sound like a jerk, and I respect your opinion, but I don't really believe that God specifically chooses which dads to present specific challenges. I think it's a bit more random than that."

"Well, regardless of what you say, God has a plan for you."

"I hope you're right. And I hope his plan includes us having a safe and fun trip to Portland. Thanks again for your kind words. And can you thank flight attendant #1 for us for being our bathroom curtain?"

"Of course. Could Alexander's dad use some ice water?"

"Yes please. That would be great. Thanks."

In a few beats, I headed back to my seat next to Alexander. Our flight attendant was a few short steps behind me carrying a two small cups of ice water and a big smile for me and my son.

Maybe God chose her to be a flight attendant for a reason.

- *Gary Dietz*

Joy

Dads of children with disabilities experience joy. Just like other dads do. Sure, sometimes our joy is highly concentrated, and we have to appreciate it quickly and deeply because it was squashed between too many other events that we may not have found particularly joyful.

But joy is indeed in the mix. Often.

We are fathers first, and we love our children and find joy in them and us and our families. Never doubt that we, our children, and our families will find joy wherever it lives. Whether that joy is dancing out in the open for all to see or hidden in a crevice where it takes some work to find.

Dads of Disability

7

Man I Can Be

Most men who find out their wife is with child become excited and start the process of planning and imagining their child's future. We ask ourselves: What kind of person will he be? What sport will she like? What kind of activities will he or she want to do? I was excited, like a child on Christmas morning.

During my wife's pregnancy, I used to sit and talk with the other guys at work and boast how strong my child would be. I wanted my child to be better and do better than me. Who wouldn't want that? My imagination ran wild with aspirations for his future. But sometimes what we imagine and what happens are dramatically different.

At six months old, Nolan was diagnosed with a rare type of epilepsy. This disability requires him to have full-time care. At first, it felt like the world was against me. I felt an overwhelming weight of guilt and frustration with all the special needs my child had. I was sad. I felt lost. And all those dreams of our future activities together seemed to drift into darkness. I was mourning for normalcy I would never have.

Nolan is now seven and in first grade. He is formally diagnosed with West syndrome, cerebral palsy, cortical visual impairment, spasticity, global developmental delay, scoliosis, and hypertension hip dysplasia. He is also non-verbal and fed using a G-tube.

Today, I'm so happy that I have reached a time in my life, as a father of a child with intense special needs, where I am proud of my son. And excited! I feel that he is becoming the person I hoped for and more.

A profound moment that I will remember forever recently occurred.

I was driving back to my house to get my laptop and passed Nolan's school. I saw children all lined up outside gathered in groups, and in one of the groups there was a wheelchair covered in camouflage. In it was a smiling boy—my boy—happy to be with friends outside. This made me very happy and proud. Tears of joy streamed down my cheeks, and I had to pull my truck over to gather my emotions.

Despite the physical pain and frustration he has endured during his life, Nolan smiles and changes people from the inside out. He does not speak a word, but he has friends who like talking to him. People are better because of him. I am a different person because he has changed me.

Through his struggles and sacrifices, Nolan has made the world a better place, and we are blessed to have such a gift in our lives. Although he has changed the world in his own way, he is not here just for others. Nolan is Nolan. He is happy to be himself for his own sake.

I have come to accept the challenges my son has. We look outside the box for activities to do with him. I feel excited about his achievements and for his future. I am very proud of the person he is becoming.

My son has changed me in a way that makes me a better man and a better father. He is the funniest person I know, and yet he does not speak one word. We enjoy all the activities I had hoped for, and he has friends and family who love him for who he is. I look forward to the future.

As the sun rises each day, Nolan and I enjoy the warmth of life. Together.

- Chas Waitt

Dads of Disability

8

55,000 Spectators

Matt was born at 11 o'clock on a very rainy night. He was 5 weeks late; weighed 9 lbs, 6 oz; and had to be delivered by caesarian section. Every time the doctor reached for him, he would pull his butt up so the doctor couldn't get a grip on him. The first, but not the only, time he would assert his independence to the world. The year was 1973, and his three siblings were waiting at home, thrilled to meet him. Everything was fine except the look on the nurse's face when I said he was beautiful. I thought nothing of it.

The next morning, I got an early call from the pediatrician as I was getting ready to go to the hospital; something about an extra chromosome. He was sorry but nothing could be done about it. I later found out that, as he was calling me, his partner was telling my wife the same thing in the hospital.

Life changed.

One example of dramatic change we noticed from the other children's births was when the doctor told us we had the option of leaving our son at the hospital. Since when was abandoning your child an option?

Fast forward six years.

Matt's older brother Ronny and I were leaving the little league field after Ronny's practice. A neighbor from two streets over whom I had never met before walked up to us, pointed at Matt, and said, "Why isn't he in a uniform?"

For the first time, I asked myself that same question. And that random act of kindness led us into the world of sports for a young man with Down Syndrome.

I wish I could say his sports career was marked with unqualified successes, but that would be a long way from the truth. However, it sent us on a journey of baseball, basketball, golf, track and field, and swimming. Those activities had some less-than-perfect outcomes. But they provided tons and tons of fun and games and achievements for Matt. And pride for all of us.

Fast forward to 1999.

We were at the Carter-Finley Stadium in Raleigh, North Carolina, for the Special Olympics. Do you know who was there? 7,000 athletes from 150 countries, 55,500 spectators, and millions of TV viewers. Plus Michael Jordan, Arnold Palmer, Billy Crystal, Stevie Wonder, Kathy Ireland, and Nadia Comaneci. And my son Matt and me. We represented the USA in the golf events. I love my other kids with all of my heart and soul, but they never put me in that crowd. Matt did!

Fast forward to now.

I am 77, and Matt is 40. He is my best friend, often my companion, and the one person I know who never says a bad word about anyone or anything. Bringing him home from that hospital all those years ago was the easiest and the best decision we ever made.

- Ron Budway, Sr.

9

Skatepark

My attitude about dads is that they need to protect their children for as long as possible based on the child's individual needs. With that in mind, it may seem that allowing my young son to walk into a skatepark, go up to an unshaven and rattily-dressed skateboarder, introduce himself, and ask in a broken sentence if he can try out his skateboard is a situation I probably wouldn't have approved of.

But here's what happened.

Skateboarder looks to Dad for permission. Dad reluctantly nods. Skateboarder says, "Sure" to Son.

Skateboarder takes one hand of Son; Dad takes the other. Son mounts skateboard. Skateboarder and Dad push Son slowly for twenty feet.

Dad prays there is no fall or cuts or sprained or broken bone or worse. (Dad imagines conversation with Son's mother based on worst-case scenario. Dad quickly ceases that line of thinking.)

Son dismounts with hands held tightly by Dad and Skateboarder. Son remounts and tries again for another twenty feet.

Son says, "All done" and dismounts skateboard. Skateboarder offers to show Son tricks.

Skateboarder shows off for about ten minutes. Impressive tricks. Son, Dad, and Skateboarder have fun doing, watching, and being watched. Time to leave.

Dad tells Skateboarder, "You are very good with my son. Thanks for being so kind." Skateboarder tells Dad, "I have a 3-year-old child with developmental disabilities. No problem. Your son is a joy."

Dad and Son walk away. Son and Skateboarder both having taught Dad a number of lessons.

- Gary Dietz

10

Great!

"Great!" my son Charlie exuberantly answered when my wife asked him how the previous night's baseball game was. It was one of the first baseball games he attended, going with his older sister and me. As is sometimes the case, he paused a bit before he answered, coming across both as a typical four-year-old kid trying to generate a thoughtful response and, to the semi-trained eye, as a kid with Childhood Apraxia of Speech (CAS).

One aspect of having apraxia is that Charlie has to first think about how to say what he wants to say. The "gr" in the word "great" is what's called a blend, a sound that two or more consonants make, which is not easy for someone with apraxia to pronounce. But he pronounced it very well. Charlie has gone from a handful of barely-intelligible words two years ago to a child who routinely impresses my wife and me with his loving, polite, witty and inquisitive talk.

It has been a lot of work, especially for him, a lot of doctor's appointments, even more therapy sessions, and still a lot more work to be done. At least receptively, Charlie's vocabulary numbers in the thousands now, yet this one-word answer meant a great deal to me, one of the joys of being a dad of disability. You appreciate the small things more—like something as simple to most as saying the word "great"—when it takes a lot of work to accomplish.

Plus, there was Charlie's typical "happiest kid on the block" tone of voice when he said it and also because of why he said it. As a dad, it's nice when your son starts to show an interest in sports. I could recount the bigger events in Charlie's life, but it's these seemingly little things that really aren't little at all.

Baseball isn't the simplest sport for a young child to understand. Try explaining a stolen base to a four year old, and you're likely to get a "did he get in trouble for stealing?" response. At times, watching a baseball game can be boring. And at times, it can be too noisy for a kid like Charlie, because he also has Sensory Integration Disorder. Short definition: loud noises *really* bother him. It's manageable and something we're working on. Charlie held up well though, and the peanuts he thoroughly enjoyed turned out to be a nice distraction.

My wife asked him why he thought the baseball game was "great." Charlie said he was really amazed by how high and far the players could hit a baseball. A high-pop fly ball that didn't reach the outfield or a routine fly-ball out that did—I can understand how a four year old can see that as amazing. Even if he didn't understand all the rules.

As delighted and amazed as Charlie was about the "great" baseball game, it couldn't compete with the delight and pride his father felt about his ability to express himself verbally. It was, as Charlie would say, "Great!"

- Douglas Keating

11

And You Made Me This

Gerard Manley Hopkins sings
Soaring songs of selving—
You read me these, rolling
Like the tides my mind sees;
I am me and free,
Singing my own song,
And you showed me this.

Common human decency
And anarchy
Share a common squiggly
As our signatures attest—
Moon lunacy, the best
Of Tristram Shandy,
And you gave me this.

See the sea through the trees,
Play of light on laughter.
Catch a fly with one hand,
No honey needed,
Get and give the giggles;
Practice *happy* forever:
And you made me this.

- Elizabeth J. (Ibby) Grace

Dads of Disability

12

Alone in the World

In the 1970s, my wife and I worked with kids with intellectual disabilities at a place called River View, which had once been a farm. Back then, there was nothing for these kids, so their parents had taken the doctor's advice and "put their child away." Many of these children were all but forgotten.

Some of the kids went home once a month, some for a holiday now and then. Those who could speak of it, did so. Absentmindedly or politely, with seeming indifference, or with the hopelessness of one buried under a bureaucracy. Some talked about it incessantly. For the others, the ones who could not speak, it was almost possible to believe they'd come from nowhere. And had nowhere to return.

And then there was Aaron. Or as he pronounced it, "Addie...Addie Rikkerds." Aaron Richards.

"...with you," he always added. "I go home with you?"

Nancy and I were hired to be houseparents in something new called a "group home." One morning, not long after we'd started at River View, the man who was supposed to be making all the arrangements took us on a little tour to one of the daycare centers and then to the Philadelphia office of the agency. Later we drove to several neighborhoods where he'd identified houses he thought would do. After that, he dropped in at River View once in a while to see how we were getting on and to tell us of his progress. Next month, he thought, things would really start to move; we should get ready.

The deal on that first house had fallen through, but he had another one lined up; it wouldn't be long. Then he had to put the second house on hold because negotiations with the city had bogged down. The months slipped by, and we began to hear from him only indirectly through the director at River View. Finally we got a letter. On all fronts, things seemed to have slowed to a crawl.

He couldn't say when the situation would change. But there was one thing we could do. Since the house would be somewhere in Philadelphia, the kids chosen for it would have to be from Philadelphia, too. And since there were many kids who fit that description now living at River View, we should start to get to know all of them and begin to think about who would come with us when the house finally opened. Aaron was one of the kids from Philadelphia.

"I go home with you?"

This was the way it was going to be. He was a little boy obsessed. If he was outside and a car he didn't recognize came up the drive, he was uncontrollable. He would break from his group and run to the driver's window, often not bothering to wait for the car to come to a stop.

"I go home with you. I go home," he'd say, shielding his eyes and peering in at the driver even before the window was rolled down.

He was seven years old, a wiry little boy in jeans and a striped T-shirt with a smile to melt lead. His black skin was dry and ashen except for the area under his wide nostrils that was alternately wet or crystal-white with dried moisture. His chin, too, was perpetually drenched. And he was in constant motion.

He'd been turned down or ignored or humored by almost every adult on the grounds of River View. But it seemed as if everyone finally gave in. Once. We heard stories of ruined chandeliers, holes in walls and closet doors, broken dishes. But we chalked much of this up to the foolishness of some of those who took him home. One newer counselor had fallen in love with him because he was so cute, and she just had to show him off.

The other seven prospects on the list we eventually drew up for our proposed group home all had some form of contact with their families, however sporadic. But Aaron was all but alone in the world.

The records we pored over in the social worker's office told us that he'd lived with his mother and grandmother for several years after he was born. But when his mother was sent to a mental health facility and with his father in jail, he was placed in a foster home. Between the ages of three and six, he had lived in seven or nine or ten foster homes. Different social workers had different ideas about counting, it seemed. Finally, his social worker at the time gave up and sent him out to River View just months before we came ourselves.

We decided that, since he'd be living with us eventually anyway, why shouldn't we start right away to provide him, as far as we could, with the support we soon hoped to be able to give him all the time when our group home opened.

We got a box spring and mattress from Nancy's mother, which we put in the back room of our apartment. And we began to bring Aaron home two weekends a month.

That first Saturday morning I woke up to the sound of walls caving in.

WHOMP! WHOMP!

5:30, the clock read.

WHOMP!

The whole apartment shook.

WHOMP! WHOMP!

The sound seemed to be coming from the back hallway. I jumped from the bed and opened the door just in time to see Aaron turning the corner.

He came toward me WHOMP! like a drunken man WHOMP! careening from one wall WHOMP! to the other.

I ran down the hall and took him by the shoulders, and the apartment stopped shaking.

"HUNG-EE!" he said, and I was sure the whole building must be awake by now.

I bent down and put my finger to my lips.

He didn't get the idea.

"I HUNG-EE!"

I put my whole hand over his mouth and bent closer to him until my eyes were in his eyes.

"SHHHHHHH!" I hissed at him almost as loudly as he had spoken.

I'd stopped him momentarily, but I could see it would only be a matter of time before he'd start up again. I was annoyed at having to get up in this way, but I couldn't be angry with him. Plainly, he was unable to control himself. He seemed oblivious to the fact that he was soaked with urine. He was finished with sleeping. The day was new, and he was ready to launch into it.

There was so much life in this little person. And all this life wanted so badly to ally itself with the other life all around it. It shouted; it banged on the walls. It told you exactly what it wanted, what it needed. It cried out, "Feed me, talk to me, play with me, teach me, help me, stay with me." "I need you," it said. "I need you. I'm all alone, and I don't want to be. Don't send me away like all the others have. Love me."

He started to holler again; and I got his attention by pressing my finger to his lips. We turned into the bathroom. I put him in the tub, started the water, and ran back to the bedroom to get his clothes, hoping he would stay until I got back. I hadn't reached the living room again before I heard his voice once more loud and strong. It wasn't that he was yelling. That is, he was yelling, by anyone else's standards. But for him communication at this volume was normal. Perhaps it was simply what he'd learn to do to make sure he wouldn't be passed over.

I ran the last steps back to the bathroom and gave him triple emphasis this time, my hand over his mouth, my finger on my own lips, and another "SHHHHHHH!"

I turned off the water and put a washcloth and a bar of soap into his hands. Then I went out to check on Nancy. It looked like she'd just woken up for the third time.

"Are you OK?" she said to the pillow in which her face was buried.

"Yeah. He needs a bath. We'll go out 'til you wake up. I don't think I can get him to be quiet."

I kept right next to him after that. I got him washed and dressed, and then we went into the kitchen. I thought we'd have breakfast first, but it was no use. He was only capable of OFF or LOUD. I put my hand over his mouth again, grabbed a few pieces of bread and our coats, and swept him out the door. The clock at the little bank up the street read 5:55.

This same scene was repeated every Saturday and Sunday that he visited—except that I set the alarm, so that I could get to him before he started down that hall. He went all day, every day, at that same pace. He was preternaturally excited. Movement called to him. He loved action of any kind. He had no quiet moments. He went full out, and when he ran out of steam, usually around 8:30 at night, he would fall asleep in an instant. In the middle of a shout, in the middle of a laugh, even standing up.

How could you help but fall in love with such vibrancy, with such life, with such straightforwardness, such honesty and goodwill? He was all I was not. He had no questions, for he knew the answers he wanted. He looked boldly outside himself for the world, for all that he needed. He had no reticence. What he could grab of life, he grabbed. And then he tried for more. His needs were as real as his appetites, clear as day and justified. His smile was as big as all his troubles. He was a little boy who'd seen a man's worth of life, and all he could tell you about it was, "Take me home!"

In those early Saturday morning hours, we walked up and down every street in that little town, and we got to know every playground and every inch of the little park. I bought him a red and yellow and blue contraption, low slung in the back, with a large plastic front wheel that scraped against the sidewalks as we went around, waiting for the rest of the world to wake up. Later, when he'd learned to ride a bicycle, I bought a used one myself, and we began to venture past the housing developments at the edge of town and out among the farms, which, back then at least, still held their own.

The first sign that the morning was progressing according to schedule was the arrival of other kids at the playground. No matter how many times I went through it, this was always a rude awakening to me. It was as if, between us, Aaron and I had managed to scrape together some semblance of a single, normal childhood. We were both sharing in this experience of childhood, but neither of us was properly equipped: he lacked the skill; I lacked the youth. Each little boy or girl we met was living an individual childhood. They were just kids. They played, went to school, had an easy life or a hard one, but a life that would be immediately understandable to one and all. But Aaron and I... What an odd pair we were: white and black, old and young, big and small, limping through the early morning streets like a creature from some other, indescribable world.

Aaron wanted to play, but he didn't really know how, and he couldn't make himself understood. When we approached all activity stopped, and the other kids all took a good, long look. There were questions, but Aaron and I together appeared so outlandish, that no words could be found for the curiosity we aroused: We were together, but what was our relationship?

"Are you his father?"

It was obvious the answer would have to be no, but I heard this question more than once: How else to make a start?

On my end I had a similar difficulty. After I'd replied in the negative, I could think of no way to describe to the questioner exactly what our relationship was. Where could I begin? "Look, kid, you got an hour...?" And so we were left standing and staring at each other, while Aaron pushed by us and onto the swings.

Though their stares didn't stop Aaron, his insistence didn't get him what he wanted either. Only rarely did we meet a child who would play with us, a child who, in fleeting innocence, saw nothing in Aaron but another playmate. How sweet those moments when I stood aside as Aaron and his newfound friend launched into the realm of play. Sometimes the little boy or girl simply swept Aaron up into something already in motion. Aaron was given the role of lighthouse in a sandbox harbor, or he was accepted as a fellow monkey on the bars. But the spell lasted only a short time before it was broken by a brother or sister or friend—or by the child himself as his natural attention turned to the next interesting thing in the immediate surroundings: Aaron and me.

But it was those brief moments of pure, uncomplicated acceptance that kept me coming back, though the inevitable end hurt the more for its delay. Those moments were the hope, the future of man, the best in man. When he saw what he needed to see and let go the misleading visions that have plagued him. When he recognized himself in all men and all men in himself.

§

When our group home finally opened, we were told that the rules had changed: Aaron could not now be one of the kids who would come to live with us, because he was from the wrong part of the city. The black part—that's what we came to understand; our group home was in a white part. But Nancy and I were not about to just forget Aaron as so many others had done before. So we found a lawyer, who found Aaron's mother and his adult sister, who, by way of responding to our request to become Aaron's legal guardians, eventually came to see us in the group home.

When we opened the front door, there was Aaron's mother along with his sister—who was decked out in the full regalia of a Black Muslim woman. I could sense that Nancy's reaction was the same as mine: "Uh-oh..." But, once they'd seen the house and met the kids who by then were living with us, the sister, Jackie, said to her mother, "This would be the best thing for him." And so we became Aaron's guardians, and he came to live with us in our apartment on the third floor and then, many years later, when both his parents had died, the three of us decided to go to court and become—officially—a family, and Nancy and I adopted Aaron.

- Karl Williams

Excerpted and adapted from a book-length manuscript.

Dads of Disability

Fear and Anger

Men can be embarrassed, angry, and fearful in the same ways as women. But we may feel and process and express those emotions differently.

If a father of a child with a disability tells you he was never afraid of something surrounding his child's disability, he is probably not telling the truth. And anger is a natural response. There is nothing wrong with a dad's anger. Even with misplaced anger, as long as it doesn't hurt anyone and the dad finds a way to work through it.

Don't ever let anyone tell a dad he is wrong for feeling a specific fear or having a specific anger. Another dad has felt the same way, too.

Dads of Disability

13

The Prosthetics Fitting Suite

With faces of burdened perplexity
they wait,
the fathers of the crippled children.

Some children loll at odd angles
in their wheelchairs,
have more hair than brain and smell

of onion sweat, of filling incontinence pads
and the false
sweetness of cleansing lotions. The fathers,

unable to help themselves, stroke the back
of their child's
head, or shoulder, or forearm, whatever

comes to hand, the repetition as
soothing
to their own selves as the watching

of waves rolling into shore,
or
the involvement in any ritual;

like coming here to wait, be measured,
the assiduous
maintenance of an orderly existence.

- Sam Smith

14

Kind of Heavy

"Son, I have something I need to talk to you about, and it's kind of heavy. That all right?"

"Yeah."

Yeah is one of Duncan's words. He has about six he can say. His cerebral palsy makes it hard for him to shape his mouth to make others, so he does the best he can with those six, although he does understand everything we say. At the time, I was helping him eat a snack of peanut butter and jelly from a bowl, washing it down with a vanilla nutrition drink. He was belted into his support chair at the table.

"Daddy's angry, son."

You see, Duncan was born four months prematurely and at the very edge of viability. He died twice his first night. We used to count the first good thing every morning thereafter as "#1: Live baby."

About the only guarantee we had in our first few weeks in the NICU was that we would swing from one emotional extreme to the other every day. During that time I learned more about my capacity to feel and my incapacity to process those feelings than in all my previous years of life and marriage.

I was terrified, of course. Afraid of what I didn't know. Afraid of what might happen to Duncan that I couldn't prevent. And afraid of making the wrong decisions for him during this critical time. I was also sad. Sad for his suffering through countless blood draws, manipulations, noise, and even exploratory surgery without anesthesia. Sad for the loss of possibilities for his future and for my inability to understand and determine outcomes for him. I was in mourning for the loss of things I never actually had—the loss of an ideal unrealized future. The loss of dreams I had for him and for me.

I was also ecstatic when things went well: When the odds broke in his favor, when we got 'the good doctor' that week. These extremes were real. Every volume knob was cranked up to 11. It was constant, real terror. Real mourning. Real grief. Real ecstasy.

Given our situation, I think all of this was understandable.

What surprised me, however, was that I was also deeply, deeply angry. Rage like that is kind of heavy. It drags you down. It caught me off guard because I'm not that guy. At least I didn't used to be. Early in our marriage, my wife actually commented that arguing with me was like arguing with Gandhi. For lack of a better term, I am Taoist in my approach to life: things happen, so make good choices based on where you are and what is. But this philosophy didn't seem to work when it came to my son and his disabilities.

Moms get angry, too, but my observations suggest that moms struggle more with grief and self-assumed guilt. My experience taught me that dads struggle more with how to love their disabled children. Not *if*, but *how*. They struggle with not being able to fix what's causing their children pain and their inability to fix the world so it doesn't matter so much that their children are disabled. I know a lot of dads struggle with having the strength to stand by their families. And I bet a lot of dads struggle with anger, too. I can't be the only one.

There at the snack table with Duncan, I had a moment of clarity.

"Son, I'm angry. I'm angry that you have CP. I'm angry that you can't see. I'm angry that you can't talk. Do you understand?"

"Yeah."

"But these things are NOT your fault. Do you hear me? NONE of those things are your fault. I'm not angry at YOU."

"Yeah."

"I just wanted you to know that. I think I also just really needed to tell you that. For me."

Duncan paused before answering for a beat longer than he usually did

"...Yeah."

Duncan is now six years old. Apart from his six words, he can't speak and communicates via noises, gestures, and a phrase flip-book we made for him to use with his hands. He lives under threat of ventricular shunt failure and seizures and is severely visually impaired. He is also strong, smart, and funny. He reads on grade level and routinely aces all his spelling tests. There is nothing wrong with his ability to think and to understand. He is a source of immense pride and inspiration for me. I don't regret any decisions I've made to help Duncan survive birth and his successive life-threatening conditions or to help him thrive despite his significant challenges. I don't consider him to be a burden or "less than."

But I'm still angry. So what do I do with that rage? The counselor in my pre-marriage sessions told me that anger is a great source of energy; it can be used as a tool to do good. So I've directed my anger at advocacy for Duncan and other children like him. I invested that energy into causes that help prevent prematurity and that support those who unavoidably find themselves in the same position as my family and me.

And you know what? It worked. I'm not less angry, but that's okay. I'm doing good things with my anger now. As a dad, having a place to put that anger where I feel it is useful has made all the difference.

Duncan gets angry sometimes, too. He rages without words, mouth screaming and hands shaking on his walker. Maybe he's angry that he can't go where he wants to right at that minute. Maybe he's angry that he can't express what he's thinking. I'm sure it's a lot of both, but perhaps it's bigger than that. Maybe he's angry at me or his mom or his cadre of doctors, therapists, teachers, and specialists. Some of them (of us) are admittedly knuckleheads. Maybe he's angry at himself because he's not like his brother or his classmates. He'll tell us when he's ready.

Duncan will grow into a man someday, sooner than I would like, and I'll be there to remind him that none of his disabilities are his fault. I'll be there to teach him that his anger is too heavy a burden to carry and that he needs to apply it somewhere outside of himself. He needs to use it to change his world in a positive way. He needs to lighten his load. Perhaps that's the most important thing any father can teach his child.

Yeah.

- Tom Lawrence

Dads of Disability

15

Helicopter Parent

In the third grade, Alexander had an assignment to dress up as a famous inventor and give a presentation to his class. At that time, one of his favorite things was helicopters. So he chose Igor Sikorsky, father of the modern helicopter, as the inventor to dress up as for his report. Because his reading and writing skills were not up to level, I wanted to help him show his classmates and his teachers that he was indeed capable.

I made a phone call to the press relations contact at the Sikorsky company and asked if there was someone who could help me get some special materials for my son's project. I told the press person about Alexander, his love of helicopters, a bit about his challenges, and what we were trying to do.

Less than a day later, I received an e-mail from Elena Sikorsky, wife of Sergei Sikorsky, Igor's son (Igor died in 1972). She let me know that Sergei would send Alexander a package with helicopter-related stuff. Soon, we received a package with a selection of trinkets and keepsakes from Sergei's attendance at an airshow in Europe as well as a copy of Sergei's biography about his father. The book was autographed for Alexander and had a hand drawing of a helicopter in the inscription.

Alexander and his mother and I worked with him using large letters and pictures in a three-ring binder to remember some sentences for his presentation. We practiced getting dressed in the Igor Sikorsky suit and hat. And drawing on a mustache. All very challenging things due to sensory issues. But we practiced and had a lot of fun and he really liked it.

The day of the presentation was a very busy one in Alexander's classroom. Lots of kids dressed up as Ben Franklin, Marie Curie, Albert Einstein, and other famous inventors. It was a very busy room, and Alexander and I left because of the commotion. I helped him prep in another room. Alexander was fairly anxiety filled. At home, he could do his presentation well. But it didn't seem like it would go as well in the classroom with all of his classmates and a lot of parents watching.

I was able to convince him to leave the room, and together, we walked back into the classroom. His mom started to videotape us. And the teacher walked us up and introduced Alexander as "Igor Sikorsky." I stood behind him to coach him on his lines, and, just before he was to start, he shrieked and then butted his head backward abruptly. Right into my nose. Crack!

In front of 25 kids, all the teachers, and a bunch of parents. On videotape. You could hear a pin drop. And Alexander saying quite emphatically "All Done!" I believe if you listened closely enough you may have heard me whimper in pain. I think my nose was fractured. It didn't bleed, but it was pretty clear that I was hurt and it was definitely sore for a few days.

This was one of my earlier lessons in meeting a child where he needs to be met. He really didn't want to do his project in front of the class. I usually pushed him maybe 10% past where he thought he could be. That is what a good dad does right? A slight, but not obnoxious, nudge to help a child learn and move forward? Push him a little outside his zone in order to learn. It usually worked. Except in this case, I guess I read him wrong and apparently pushed him a bit beyond his usual comfort zone.

So, after proving to half of the third grade parents in our small town that I could take a hard head butt to the nose and gracefully exiting the room with Alexander, we decided to adapt Alexander's project in an edited video. We taped it at home, I edited it, and he showed it to his class. We enjoyed dressing up again, making the video, and he enjoyed watching his classmates watch his video. We also sent the video to Sergei and Elena Sikorsky.

My son, within one degree of separation from the inventor of the modern helicopter. And me, with a sore nose and an evolving perspective on parenting.

- Gary Dietz

Dads of Disability

16

Inveterate

One day folds to the next,
Tuesday becomes Wednesday
with no more to mark it
than another row gone
in the medicine box,
a slight change of wording
in the daily petition:

Let us make it to Thursday
without getting hurt,
without calling the sheriff
to gentle an illness
that's already killed us.

- Patricia Wallace Jones

Dads of Disability

17

Man Up

"Man up!"

I have heard myself say those words many times.

I am far from the stereotype of a big manly man, for whom testosterone is a sacred thing. I am, however, a former Marine Corps Sergeant, and that has impacted me deeply. When I am pushed to extremes, I fall back on that training, most of which can be boiled down to: "Man up and do what you have to do!"

The extremes I get pushed to most frequently are related to my son. Alex is a wonderful, genius-level, funny, and kind-hearted young man. He is also diagnosed with bipolar disorder, oppositional defiance disorder, and emotional disorder NOS (not otherwise specified). Thanks for the clarity on that last one, Doc.

When Alex is stable, he is great to be around. But that stability is brittle, and the whole family knows that the slightest misstep can result in an avalanche of fury, self loathing, outward aggression, and misery. And when those storms come, when the last reserves of my own emotional restraints slip, I fall back into Sergeant mode and begin to give orders.

My voice is deep and carries a long way, both in the house and in time. I can see my son flinch when I remember saying:

"How are you going to survive? If you can't even deal with socks that don't fit right, how can you deal with anything?"

"Not everything is about you! Sometimes you just need to man up and do what you are told!" (There it is.)

"I need you to obey me. Now, just do it!"

Telling someone who is already at a low ebb of bipolar/ODD to obey you is quite possibly the stupidest tactic you can take. It's like telling a shark to ignore something bloody floating in the water. It guarantees that the fight is about to get nasty.

So Alex digs into his emotional toolbox and finds the things he knows hurt the most. He was hurt because I didn't believe in him and because I questioned his imminent manhood, I think. So he wields his genius intellect with the strength of sadness and outrage and says and does the things that hurt my wife, my daughter, my father, and especially me. Even if the things he says and actions he takes hurt him, too, he says and does them anyway.

The Marine in me understands the impulse. I pushed his back to the wall with my inability to back down or try a more sophisticated tactic. In his mind, I gave him no recourse but to fight back. But then he pushes my back to the wall, and I fight back, too.

Now, the world my family lives in is a war zone, and repairing the damage when the shooting stops is very hard and never complete. Like the European cathedrals that survived World War II only to carry scars and bullet holes into the future.

Sitting here, in the quiet of my office, I can be more or less clinical. I can say "Yes, when he does X and I do Y, that results in Z." But when Alex, a young man who is approaching adulthood, challenges me or threatens the rest of my family, logic seems irrelevant. I become a fighter again. I become the Sergeant who must be obeyed. And the battle starts again.

I realize that my son is not the only one who should be told to man up. And that is not at all a pleasant thought.

The questions keep me awake: How do I prepare Alex for manhood if I can't get him to deal with simple problems? If disappointment over how well the WiFi is working can throw him into a tailspin, how can I hope that he will be able to deal with the rigors of a job? Will he ever be strong enough to face life without us?

Those are not foreign concerns for any parent; I have to remind myself of that. But the developmental path his problems put in front of us leaves us without a clear roadmap. We don't get to fall back on the reassurance that it's just a phase.

If I admit that strong-arming him into mature behavior is not going to work and that little else seems to break through, I have to come to grips with the notion that manhood as I have defined it may never happen for him. My wife and I have talked about the need to just build a little cabin in the back yard, so at least he always has a home.

But even that is hard. I feel the scorn of other parents. I hear the voices of my grandparents (none of whom really even met Alex) deriding me for being so bad at manhood myself that I could not pass it on to my son. Those are my own demons. I get that, but they are there nonetheless, telling me to push him harder than I should.

My conversations with God sound almost identical to my son's conversations with me. I whine, I plead, I rage. All to get what I want, which is a son who can continue when I am gone.

At the end of the day, I love Alex. His flaws are just magnifications of my own, which is why they enrage me so. Thus, I will continue to try, to love, to take a ten-minute break instead of pushing the point for a resolution right now. And I may begin investigating the process of adding a cabin in the back. He's my son, after all. And taking care of him is what a man is expected to do. So I will man up and do it. Even when it seems impossible.

- Hal Hanlin

18

The iPod

Herman stepped gingerly onto the bus—
a forty-five year old man, backpack
low slung cinching the tweed overcoat
that overhung his unclasped galoshes.
He fingered the cleft of his oval plastic
coin purse for quarters and dimes.
Inspected each face for blemishes before
dropping the shiny coins in the slotted
glass box for passage. Shuffled his way

to the back of the bus, past the taunts
and sneers, derision, the unmuffled
laughter. He'd hear, "Here comes
the retard." But Herman looked straight
down at his feet scraping the corrugated
rubber running the length of the bus.
He tripped over one of the hoodlum's
legs stuck out as he neared, and tumbled,
arms spread as if flailing wings for a brief
uncontrolled flight. He crashed into arms
of another ne'er-do-well perched at the end
of the rubber runway—the iPod took-off
from his hands, flew into an aluminum pole
deflecting hard into metal rails, breaking-up
into inoperative hunks of lifeless electronics.

"Sorry, sorry" he said, picking himself up.
The angry punk grabbed Herman by the
collar of his coat and shook him spitting
epithets. An older guy in shirt & tie,
horn-rimmed glasses, absorbed in a Wall
Street journal, stood up
for Herman, exchanged his Clark Kent
demeanor for a couple of steel fists
to the jaws of harassing thugs;
martialled his legs to their chests.

Meanwhile, in a quieter corner
of the flat-gray bus, Herman tinkered
with the broken pieces,
laid them on the dark green cushion
in the back of the bus. His backpack, full
of what-nots and thingamajigs, crazy glue,
wire on a spool, batteries, tweezers
and a Swiss-made pocketknife with mini
screwdrivers and a rasping awl. His tools,
he deftly wielded despite the rumblings
from diesel engine coming through the seat.

He dismantled the iPod cover
hiding the dead circuits; resurrected them
with ingeniousness—a spot welding device:
battery and shorted wires to solder
the wire paths broken in the fall.
When he finished, he polished

the bandaged iPod with his shirt.
The screen brightened with a song
list again and the music played
through the earphones.

The bus driver had called the police;
they came with their billy clubs
in about ten minutes, but the older guy
didn't need any of their help. The punks
complained of Herman's intentional
destruction of the iPod. But the faint
sound of a Rolling Stones' song
spilled out through the earphone
as Herman handed the good-as-new
iPod to the officer... without looking
into his eyes; and the words of
Mr. Jimmy and Mick Jagger chimed out—
something about not always getting
what you want, but if you try
you might get what you need.

They hauled the hoodlums off to jail.
Herman neatly tucked his tools away.
When he came home, his eyes narrowed,
and he said, "Pop, I need a gun,
a soldering gun."

- *John C. Mannone*

Dads of Disability

Admiration

It's one thing for a stranger to tell a dad, "You are doing a great job" or that they are a "hero." Those are nice things to say, but really, we are just being fathers. And, even if we are indeed going "above-and-beyond," what exactly does that mean? Above-and-beyond what? What is the alternative?

It's another thing to follow Dale Carnegie's excellent rules of giving sincere and honest and specific compliments. A compliment that takes specific detail and context into account is more meaningful—for all parents.

This section features a number of women who share specific stories of deep and authentic admiration of the dads of disability in their lives.

Dads of Disability

19

The Cold Side of the Bed

Every morning, long before the break of dawn, I wake to find the other half of our marriage bed cold and empty. That might sound strange coming from a woman who has been faithfully married to the same man for more than three decades.

Early in our special needs parenting experience, I'd get resentful about that pre-dawn vacancy. That cold, unoccupied spot signified that my husband slept well enough the previous night to wake early and start a new day. Usually, I wasn't as fortunate. My sleep was almost always disturbed by tossing and turning from worry about both of the children's IEPs, therapies, appointments with specialists, meetings with schools, and the never-ending self-education in which I was absorbed.

I resented that my husband went to his career of choice every day while my career as advocate, therapist, disability expert, taxi driver, mediator, and special education lawyer was chosen for me by default, with me kicking and screaming all the way! He could be a regular dad. Why couldn't I be a regular mom?

I also resented little things. On his 45-minute drive to work, he could listen to anything he wanted to on the stereo. As loud as he pleased. I, on the other hand, would be subjected to distracting tantrums if the same, familiar CD wasn't playing in the car as I toted my children to therapy and other appointments at various locations across the state.

I resented his cold side of the bed as a symbol of his "convenience of escape." Like a thief in the night, he could rise out of bed, leave me in the dark with all the family problems, and escape with no accountability. He was the almighty bread winner! And at some level, I really couldn't argue with that. We needed to eat and have a roof over our heads. He had a perfectly valid reason to escape, but if I had done the same (as I'd fantasized about doing so many times), my reasons for defection wouldn't have been so honorable.

I felt alone in the responsibility of parenting two children with disabilities. It was so overwhelming at times that I just wanted to scream. I wanted to hand it all over, with confidence, to someone who could carry the load for a bit because my husband wasn't there. He was out winning the bread all the time and leaving our house as early as he could to get away from us.

Or so I thought.

One morning, I couldn't get back to sleep after his 3 a.m. alarm. So I slipped quietly downstairs and observed him in the dark, sipping a cup of coffee. He was just sitting, with no distractions, rocking back and forth in his reclining chair. After a few moments, I asked him if he was OK.

He replied that he did this every morning. That this was his way of thinking things through. That he enjoyed the quiet and solitude and needed the time to clear his head. He also reasoned that he would rather work overtime by rising at an ungodly hour and getting to work before other staff and distractions showed up. That way he could always be home on time in the evenings to be with the kids.

And he always was.

This man who worked so hard and carried his own burdens was creating a pause of peace that didn't cut into the time he was able to spend with his family. He chose to sit awake and alone to reflect and recharge. This was his way of being at his best for his family. While I craved a few more hours in bed in hopes of functioning the next day, he chose the dark solitude of early morning to do the same.

§

We have gained tremendous wisdom as special needs parents through the years. It hasn't always been pretty, but we've always come out the other side on the same team. My husband learned how to advocate for himself as an employee and adopted the "my family comes first" rule as our children grew. More and more, he accompanied me to meetings, specialist appointments, and learned how to just listen when I had to unload. He faced difficult social challenges in the community with our children. He resolved that he didn't always have to "fix" a problem I was experiencing. He learned it was often enough just to hold my hand as I raved.

I have also matured a great deal over the years. This is due in large part to my husband's patience with me, his ability to live in the moment with his kids, and his reassurance that "we can get through anything together." I've also learned that I'm not always right about things (gasp!) and that there is no shame in admitting that.

Recognition of one's own fallibility truly adds inches to the "personal growth chart."

In hindsight, I can see how difficult those early years must have been for my husband. Not only was he a dad, he was a mate to a strong-willed woman and a provider for a complex family. How conflicted he must have felt when I was out of my mind with fear, grief, and uncertainty! I know he wanted to be with me at those times, but he also needed to bring home the bacon for his children and wife. It couldn't have been an easy line to walk. Navigating those roles in a typical family are enough to tap out the average person. Put disability on top of it (in our case, times two!), and it takes a real man to stick with it and figure out how to make it work. I have enormous respect for my husband and don't know another man like him. His evolution to a man of integrity has truly been the result—a gift, really—of being a dad of disability.

§

All these years later my husband still wakes at an ungodly hour. While I still wish he'd choose to sleep longer for health reasons, his early-morning solitude is no longer a source of resentment for me. Now, the cold side of the bed represents the source of warmth, security, and consistency provided by the amazing man my children call "Dad."

- *Viki Gayhardt*

20

The Right Thing

When I first met my husband, he struck me as extraordinarily kind. He was soft spoken and unusually shy, but quite bright. I liked his predictability. He got up at the same time every morning, ate the same breakfast every day, and walked the same route to work, stopping along the way for a bagel and coffee. He worked in a small office and got along quite well with his middle-aged supervisor.

He was dependable and predictable. When we went out to eat, he even ordered the same meal every time. When he took vacation, he went back to his "old haunts." Each day of the week had its own scheduled routine, including clothing, meals, and activities.

I had never met anybody like him in my life. For a girl like me, a writer and artist, he was a welcome change. I'd had my heart broken a few times, and he was safe.

We got married and had two daughters. My first daughter was what we called "high maintenance." She was cranky all the time. Even as an infant, she demanded my constant attention, and I couldn't figure out why she was so easily irritated. The first time I held her and tried to nurse her, I noticed that she had one noteworthy reflex: she could flail her arm.

And flail it she did, with all her might. At me. Until she turned bright red with anger.

Over time, I became convinced that my baby didn't like me. From the start, it took very little to send her into a full-blown tantrum—a strange smell, the sun in her eyes, or a pair of socks or leggings that didn't feel right. While her behavior was within the normal range for toddlers, she never outgrew the tantrums and flailing of her arms. She began to hit (usually me.) When she entered elementary school, I began to worry. And then, with a new baby in the house, it was difficult to keep them both safe.

My second daughter had similar sensitivities, only more remarkable. She was especially sensitive to sound, and the whistle of a tea kettle or the honk of a horn seemed torture to her. As soon as she was able, she began covering her ears.

Looking back at this time, I can see that my daughters began to show me what bothered them, but I didn't understand. They would not let me bathe them or brush their hair. They could not tolerate certain foods, bright lights, clothing with tags, socks, loud noises, supermarkets, or malls. They had difficulty sleeping. They were prone to tantrums and hitting. Oddly, though, what would soothe them one day would irritate them beyond measure the next.

"Leave them alone," my husband would say. "They're like cats. You have to let them come to you."

I didn't get it. These were my children; they grew in my body. How could I leave them alone?

Chaos became the natural result of the effort it required to modify their world to their idiosyncrasies. To care for them, my husband and I had to let everything else go. We slept little, ate poorly, and bickered often. My husband began to shut down. His routine was his comfort, and the children disrupted that routine. He became angry and sullen. Suddenly, I was the problem.

"You're like a dog, Elizabeth," he told me. "You get in their space. You want to play and rough house with them. But they're cats. They don't like that."

I had no idea what he was talking about.

At eight years of age, my oldest daughter was a wreck. Her hair was matted to her head, she wore the same clothes every day, and she refused to bathe. She slept in pull-ups. My four year old had speech delays, was not potty trained, and could not sleep alone. They panicked and threw tantrums when I dropped them off at school or day care. I worried about them constantly and subsequently took them to play therapy.

My children began to echo their father. "Leave us alone, Mom. Why do you have to tell everyone our problems?"

Yet, I couldn't leave them alone. Something was wrong, and I didn't know what it was. And deep down, at the core of me, I felt that it had to be somebody's fault. I was the only one seeing a problem, and my gut instinct told me it was more than just cats and dogs. I thought if only I could work with them alone, get them away from their father, that I would be able to help them. Exasperated and exhausted, I filed for divorce.

I managed as a single parent for a while, but I longed to remarry. I felt that the girls needed a man, a father figure. Naively, I believed that a strong male presence in their lives would ground them and help to stabilize us all. So I married a military man who loved structure, authority, and schedules. But despite both our efforts, everything got much, much worse.

Both children were placed on medication. When medication failed to help, they were hospitalized and subsequently placed in residential treatment. We began family therapy—all five of us—and the repercussions were dramatic. My second marriage faltered and then expired; I had chosen the wrong father figure.

The lessons were painful and profound. First, I have learned that my daughters don't need a father. They need their father. They need to see him, talk to him, and be in the same room with him every day. This is a fact. I don't have to like that fact or even understand it, but I do have to accept it.

Furthermore, I erroneously believed that I knew my children better than their father—because I was educated, because I had given birth to the girls, and because I am a woman. They grew in my body, after all. But it turns out that while I may have some insight about them, their father does, too. He sees things in them that I don't see, and he knows things about them that I couldn't possibly know—not because he's a man, but because he is their father. My daughters have 23 of his chromosomes and 23 of mine. They are half him and half me.

Finally, I've learned that my ex-husband and I are parents of two girls on the autism spectrum. My ex-husband has Asperger's Syndrome, too. Regrettably, our marriage didn't work out. But to meet the extraordinary needs of our daughters, we share a living space and expenses, much like married people. On many days, I am uncomfortable, but I show up to do what is needed. I cooperate and raise them with their father because it is what they need, and it is the right thing to do. That lesson is ongoing, expanding, and evolving.

- Elizabeth O'Neill

Dads of Disability

21

A Father's Unbroken Vow

When we found out we were pregnant, my husband Ryan and I made an appointment to see a genetics counselor. She interviewed us and was especially interested in Ryan's medical history.

Born with normal hearing, Ryan soon had a bilateral, profound level of deafness. This was the result of an elevated temperature from influenza when he was nine months old. His younger brother also became deaf when he was twelve months old after a high temperature from the flu. Ryan's mother became deaf when she was three years old after complications from the measles. His father and older brother had normal hearing.

Ryan signed the release forms, and his medical records were collected and compiled.

At the next appointment, we were told, "Your baby has a fifty-percent chance of being born deaf and a fifty-percent chance of going deaf between birth and adulthood." On the ride home, I prayed, "God, please keep Your hands on my baby's little ears."

At home, we sat at the kitchen table and had coffee. Ryan signed, "I'm excited. I hope our baby is born deaf, deaf like me."

I signed "What?" in an exaggerated way, to show my disbelief. "Are you serious? You want your child to be deaf? And miss out on so much in life?"

"Couples with brown hair and brown eyes want the same for their babies," he signed. "It's normal to want your children to be like you. It makes parents feel proud. You want a hearing child, don't you?"

I raised my hand and signed, "Yes."

"A hearing child will live in your hearing world, but a deaf child will be part of my Deaf world."

I tried to talk with him about this but couldn't. I didn't know this selfish Deaf man who thought only of himself! I thought we shared a world. I didn't understand why he wanted our child to be deaf. It bewildered me. Why didn't he tell me this before? Why didn't I ask?

For the first time, I wondered if our bilingual, bicultural marriage was a mistake. Later, in bed, I wondered if I was as selfish as Ryan because I wanted a hearing baby. I started to pray. But what was the use? Ryan's prayers and mine would cancel each other out.

The next weekend we went to Deaf Club, where voicing was not permitted. I was the only hearing member present. Our Deaf friends gathered and signed, "Baby... deaf?... Hearing..." Each person who asked told us they hoped our baby is born deaf. Some crossed their fingers to wish us luck. Not *one* person asked if we knew if our baby was a boy or a girl, or which names we were considering. While all deaf people may not want deaf children, the people in my small world certainly seemed to.

I loved Ryan. I tried harder to understand his Deaf world. Our communication improved, and we openly discussed the possibilities we might face as parents. We both vowed to trust God, and unconditionally accept and love the child He gave us.

Ryan signed stories to my bulging belly as the delivery date approached. After thirty-six hours of hard labor and an emergency caesarian under anesthesia, we greeted baby Barbara. An interpreter came to the hospital at 4 a.m. to help Ryan and the team communicate. Ryan managed post-caesarian details, while I slept in the recovery room.

The following day, Barbara's pediatrician met with Ryan and me. "We gave Barbara three hearing tests. She passed two of them. She may be hard of hearing, but I'm positive she isn't profoundly deaf at this time." He referred us to a specialist.

Thank God Barbara could hear.

Later, they brought Barbara to my room. I held her close, kissed her forehead, signed and said, "I love you." I handed her Ryan. He cuddled her close to his chest. To test her hearing, I quickly clapped my hands over her head. Barbara jerked slightly. So did Ryan—not because he heard me, but because he was shocked. He furiously signed with one hand, holding Barbara with the other.

"No more of that! If she's not deaf now, she will be by the time you're done!" Sarcasm works in American Sign Language, too.

We soon followed up with the referral to a specialist. As far as he could tell, Barbara's hearing was normal. He instructed us to watch her closely for fevers and to treat temperatures over 100 degrees Fahrenheit as an emergency and go to the ER. "I'll draft a letter explaining Ryan's family history of deafness you can take with you."

Barbara had her first elevated temperature when she was three months old. The ER doctor medicated her, ran lab work, and kept her overnight for observation. The origin of her fever was determined to be a common cold, and she retained her hearing.

Ryan and I both worked: he as a cabinet maker and I as a family therapist. Two days a week I worked evenings. Those evenings, after work, Ryan picked Barbara up from my mother's, took her home, and cooked supper. Some of our hearing friends expressed concern that Ryan couldn't hear Barbara cry, might not recognize the symptoms of a fever, or know how to communicate with medical professionals.

I was completely confident in Ryan's ability and planning to care for Barbara and never considered him an inferior parent because of his deafness. We had a TDD, a telecommunication device for the deaf that looked like a small typewriter with a micro printer. Ryan wired a baby monitor to his visual alert system and our telephone and doorbell to gigantic strobe lights on the walls throughout our house. They flashed in different patterns to alert Ryan when the phone rang or when someone was at the door. When they were activated, blinding lights flashed, bouncing off walls, and the house lit up like a disco on a busy Saturday night.

Ryan's primary mode of communication was American Sign Language, his ability to speechread severely limited. He signed with Barbara; I signed and spoke with her. We often played Christian children's music or turned on *Sesame Street* for additional stimulation to help her with language development.

"Daddy" was Barbara's first word in baby sign language, followed by "cookie," and then "mommy." She was six months old. The following month, she voiced "mama" and "dada" for the first time

There was a consensus among professionals we knew in the Deaf community and in my circle of health-care colleagues that Barbara would naturally speak with speaking people and sign with deaf people. We were advised that children intuitively know that oral English and American Sign Language are two distinct languages, and when to use them. But it wasn't so in Barbara's case. At age two, Barbara expected everyone to know and use sign language. When she didn't want to sign, she closed her eyes. When she didn't want to talk, she covered her ears. She was often frustrated with other hearing children who didn't sign.

When she was four, we enrolled her in a small Christian preschool where she could receive individualized attention. They gently reminded her to use her voice when she signed. Within a month, she was consistently talking with hearing children at school.

In social settings, Ryan and I helped Barbara understand who in the room spoke, signed, or did both. If she forgot, we calmly reminded her again. By the first grade, she knew when to speak and when to sign. Always curious, she'd often ask hearing people why they couldn't talk with their hands and deaf people what was wrong with their ears.

Ryan and I remained circumspect and continued to treat Barbara's elevated temperatures as emergencies. She had a history of chronic middle-ear infections that caused high fevers. Tympanostomy tubes (also known as grommets) were implanted in her eardrums to prevent the accumulation of fluid, with positive results. Once, Barbara lost fifty percent of her hearing in her left ear due to an unusual wax buildup. It was easily treated, and her hearing returned to normal.

Our ultimate parental challenge was when Barbara was seven and had chicken pox. Her pediatrician prescribed a fever-reducing regimen and told us to stay by her side— that her risk for deafness was increased. Ryan and I took a week off work and maintained a bedside vigil. We prayed, and asked others to pray. I resisted the urge to startle her while she slept to test her hearing. It felt surreal that Barbara could wake up deaf as Ryan, her uncle, and her grandmother had. Especially after hearing for seven years.

Barbara is now 25, and her hearing is normal. She has Lupus and has had several elevated temperatures from pneumonia and bronchitis due to her compromised immune system. Her doctors tell her they hope her risk for deafness has passed, but they can't be certain. We are told her future children have a twenty-five percent risk of being born deaf or going deaf after an elevated temperature. (Additional risk will depend on the future father's risk factors for deafness.)

§

Prior to Ryan's death a few years ago, we had several conversations about his desire to have a deaf child. I understood how Barbara's path created numerous detours from Ryan's Deaf world. He never heard her laugh with her friends, cry for help, or sing on stage. He had no hearing frame of reference for her love of music or dancing, though he was always supportive of her. (It probably wasn't his deafness that caused an issue with dancing. He just didn't like dance!) Ryan stretched and tried to be part of her hearing world.

Never once did Ryan say he wished Barbara was the deaf child he hoped for, though I can see the difference it would have made in his life. I deeply regret not understanding how normal his feelings were and that I judged him so harshly. I asked Ryan to forgive me, and he did.

For his entire life, Ryan kept his pregnancy vow. He trusted God, and unconditionally accepted and loved the child He gave us.

- Pam Hauck

Dads of Disability

22

Scenes from a Marriage

Yesterday afternoon, I poked my head into the family room where Jack, Charlie, and Henry were sprawled watching Scooby Doo and announced we were going for haircuts. "No!" they shouted in unison. "No haircuts!" I told them we'd stop at the school book fair first and jollied them out the door with promises of new joke books and Batman stories.

About forty-five minutes later, we pulled into the barbershop parking lot, and Jack began to whimper and whine. As I opened the van door, his agitation accelerated, and he refused to get out of the car. Wow, I thought to myself. He's really off today. I scanned my mental list of things that typically contribute to Jack's "offness"—bad night of sleep, hunger, dog sighting—but couldn't come up with a reason. "A haircut will give me a headache!" he repeated over and over.

Once I finally got him out of the car, he wouldn't come inside. He stood outside kicking the door with a blue sneaker while the patrons waiting inside exchanged glances. I told him brightly that his favorite stylist, Terri, was here, and she was going to cut his hair like she always does. Then I gritted my teeth, bent close to his ear, and hissed that I would take every one of his books back if he didn't come in the door this minute.

"It will hurt!" he raged. "I will have a HEADACHE from this haircut!"

We waited for a little bit, and just as it was Jack's turn to climb into the chair, my husband Joe walked in to drop Joey off on the way to another family errand. Jack started to throw an epic tantrum, jumping and crying and twirling like a tornado.

I looked over my shoulder as Joe started out the door, asking for help with my eyes. He walked back in and took Jack by the shoulders, directing him towards the large, black barber chair as Jack screamed and flailed. I backed away, letting Joe handle the moment, and made nervous conversation with a mom who was waiting with her two sons.

In the midst of the chaos, Joe and Terri discovered a giant spot of dried hair gel behind Jack's left ear. I remembered the day before how he'd disappeared into the bathroom and came out with his hair slicked and sticky; he must not have washed it all out during his nightly shower. And he was terrified it would hurt.

Slowly, they maneuvered him towards the sink, promising they could wash it out. But Jack was lost to any reason—agitated and deregulated and just plain out of his mind. He kept sitting up and getting water everywhere. I heard an edge in Joe's voice and decided to step in, to declare "game over." This did not go over well with my husband, and when we got home, we launched into an epic argument.

And our epic argument made Jack's tantrum seem like child's play, as we waged our war of *how could you not see that giant gob of gel in his hair* and *why don't you try taking him for haircuts and doing homework with him every night*. A war of the always and the never: *you always undermine me* and *you never hear him when he's screaming*.

Joe's first instinct in a stressful situation (he is a man, after all) is to try and solve the problem, to create a solution. *Boy needs haircut! Gel in hair! Wash gel out!* (I didn't mean for this line to come out so caveman-like! Honest!) I am very sensitive to Jack's distress, to the screams of *the water is running down my back* and *those scissors will hurt*. In most cases, Joe's practical yin to my emotional yang works very well. He stays focused on the task at hand while I soothe and pacify. And the hair gets cut.

But not this time.

I believe sometimes kids can bring out the worst in a marriage. Like miniature construction workers with teeny-tiny pick axes, they chip away at your foundation until there are huge, gaping cracks. Five kids can do a lot of damage if you aren't careful. And when one of the children has a disability, it can make a marriage even more challenging.

So Joe and I went round and round with our verbal jabs and punches as if we were boxers in a ring, ducking and dancing like Rocky and Apollo. But instead of Mick and Adrienne and that guy Rocky used to work for on the docks watching us, our spectators were four boys and a girl. And their eyes were as round as saucers.

"You no SHOUT! You hurt ME EARS!" Henry refereed. We paused momentarily to tell them Mommy and Daddy are just having a *disagreement*. We are fine. It's no different from the way they fight with each other over Legos and Matchbox cars and who got the last purple popsicle.

"We never fight like this," Charlie whispered conspiratorially to Joey.

"Why don't you get DIVORCED already," was Jack's contribution.

The irony of the interactions in the barbershop and how we reacted is not lost on me. I mean, I was interviewed by FOX News, spouting off academic truths like *behavior always has purpose* and *try to understand what motivates*. Meanwhile, I completely missed the practical reason Jack didn't want to get a haircut: he was afraid the scissors would pull on all that flaky, white gel, and it would hurt his head. That's why he kept telling me a haircut would give him a headache.

I'm concerned that some people may interpret my media messages and blog and book to mean my husband Joe and I have a "handle" on autism, and that we help Jack thrive flawlessly and effortlessly. But we don't. Just when the seas feel calm and the wind is quiet, there is a sudden violent squall, and Joe and I are left reeling, wet and shivering in the cold. And then, like many married couples, when we aren't careful, we turn on each other.

The truth is, ours is a life of a thousand frustrations. Just like the lives of millions of married couples with kids. However, with a disabled child, emotions and reactions can be magnified a thousand fold. Sometimes we fight; sometimes we cry. We are always trying to find better ways to communicate when a storm sweeps over us. It would be much easier to share only the bright spots of our family and marriage with the outside world: the license plate games, the trips to Cancun, the family karate, and the moments of tenderness Joe and I show each other that may be deeper than most because of how much we go through together. But showing only happy faces would not be real. And so I offer you our imperfect life, our imperfect marriage, a public nod of respect to Joe. I offer a life bursting with joy and frustration, of flowing tears and fragrant trays of chocolate chip cookies warm from the oven.

I offer you our family's truth, our marriage reality show. Sometimes it is raw and fragile. Like now.

After a fitful night of sleep, I woke to a cool, gray day. I wanted to curl under the covers and sleep until noon. I wanted to pack up all of Joe's clothes—his ugly flannel shirts from college, his new dress pants from Banana Republic—and throw them down the stairs for dramatic flair. I wanted to cry.

But I didn't do any of these things. Instead, I went through the motions and the mechanics of our life. I toasted waffles and went to the gym and waved to the teacher in the preschool line. And slowly, like winter turning to spring, I started to thaw.

Will we get divorced? Probably not. We will do what we always do; we will return to one another. With a brush of our hands or a quick smile over something funny Henry says at dinner, we will move forward. Joe's dark brown eyes will twinkle, and he'll share a small joke as a peace offering.

We will forgive each other and help each other forgive ourselves.

Because it was Joe who was there to hear me say *something is wrong* as we sat on our old brown couch in

Buffalo, talking and worrying about Jack late into the night. He was the one I called to shout *he said mama just now mama.* In my darkest moments of frustration and fear, Joe is the one I need the most. And in times of happiness and joy, we celebrate. Together.

- Carrie Carriello

23

Dadaptation

My husband Cliff is an electronics engineer who claims he can fix anything using a crate of tomatoes, bailing wire, and super glue. And over the years, he's shown us he can.

Our third child and first son, Kevin, was born in 1988 at 29 weeks gestation. Today that doesn't seem like a big deal, but back then it was pretty serious. I was told our baby boy only had a thirty-percent chance of survival, and if he survived, he would have multiple physical and medical problems for the rest of his life. Well, he survived and does indeed have serious physical and medical issues.

However, for Kevin, the positive things in his life outshine those challenges. He's always been our "can do kid." Before Kevin came along, our family loved boating, camping, biking, and generally being outdoors. When Kevin was diagnosed with severe cerebral palsy at two years of age, we didn't stop doing any of those things. We just did them differently.

After Kevin was diagnosed, I knew that Cliff would use his fix-it skills to adapt stuff to make it work for Kevin. Once Cliff tore down an old motorized wheelchair and turned it into a slow, but workable, go-cart for Kevin. I'm not sure who had more fun with that one: Kevin, his friends, or Cliff!

Recently, Cliff even adapted our family travel trailer to make a "private bedroom" for Kevin. Now an adult, Kevin can easily get into the trailer and from his wheelchair to bed and back. And he has the privacy to do his own thing while the rest of the family chills. Cliff's project has really made camping an easier venture for all of us.

I am in awe of Cliff and what he does for Kevin. But so far, none of the things I have shared with you put Kevin or anyone else in peril.

§

When Kevin was in the fourth grade, he really wanted to be in the Boy Scouts. Cliff and some other dads who had been in the Indian Guides program decided to transition the boys from Guides to Scouts. Kevin loved the adventure, the idea of being "prepared," and the camp outs. Soon Kevin was invited by a friend of his sister's to bridge into a Boy Scout troop. (This friend was Kevin's inspiration for later working for and attaining the rank of Eagle Scout! Another amazing accomplishment, but a different story.)

Kevin and his dad often traveled with his troop to a Boy Scout camp about a four-hour drive from where we live. Kevin loved the one-on-one time with Dad (in other words, being away from Mom) as much as he loved the outdoors. He knew he was going to get to do stuff I would never approve of. With Dad, he got to have a snake wrapped around his neck, shoot a rifle, go sky sailing, hike to the top of a mountain to see a fire lookout, and ride a zip line. If I'd gone, we probably would have spent the week basket weaving.

Here are three perspectives on one such camping trip. I believe I mentioned peril?

The Dad: Cliff's Point of view

When I was approached by the leadership of the Scout camp about letting ten-year-old Kevin zip line as part of an emergency evacuation exercise, I was all for it. The process for that particular experience included hauling him up to the top of a rickety fire lookout-type structure, hooking him up to a harness, hooking him up to another harnessed Scout leader, and then shoving them off the structure. There was a team of Scouts at the bottom to catch them, and all went well.

A couple of years later, they wanted to let Kevin have the zip line experience again, but this time they got really creative. We designed a platform, more like a sled, that an older Scout and Kevin could be strapped to in addition to their harnesses. It looked safe enough to me.

They got Kevin staged, and one of Kevin's friends got the video camera ready. It looked pretty good until about 20 or 30 feet from the end of the ride, when the "sled" started to disintegrate. By the time the thing stopped, Kevin was hanging upside down, and it looked like his head had slammed into a rock!

All hell broke loose while Scouts were yelling for first aid and trying to untangle Kevin and the other Scout from the twisted remains of the structure. They used all the training Scouts go through to be prepared for accidents out in the middle of nowhere. When Kevin was finally untangled from it all, he grinned. And in typical Kevin style innocently asked, "Can we do it again?" Everyone busted up laughing.

Fortunately nobody got hurt, and I quickly told Kevin, "Don't you dare tell your mom!"

The 12 year-old Scout: Kevin's Point of view

I was so excited about getting to do a zip line again. I thought it was overkill building a special "sled" for me to ride in, but when my dad gets involved, you pretty much have to go with the plan.

The worst part of the whole ordeal was getting hauled up onto the platform where the zip line starts. But once I was up there, they strapped me and the older Scout onto the thing, and we were ready to go. They pushed us off, and wow, what a ride!

As we got closer to the end, I could feel things starting to come apart. The next thing I knew I was hanging upside down staring at a rock. I really couldn't figure out what all the commotion was about. I wasn't hurt, and the other Scout and I were just cracking up. I really wanted to go again, but one look at our totaled ride and I knew that wasn't going to happen. I mostly remember Dad telling me, "Don't tell Mom!"

The Mom: Bobbie's Point of view

I worried when the boys went off to camp. There was always some adventure like a story about a rattle snake, some treacherous hike, or how bad the food was. This time was no different.

I knew something was up when, on the day they were headed home, Cliff called me to tell me they were on the road. I asked how it went, and Cliff kept assuring me over and over again that Kevin was fine! Of course I said, "And why wouldn't he be?" He replied, "Nothing to worry about, Kevin's fine!" This gave me something to think (worry?) about for the next few hours.

When they got home, they both had sort of a sheepish look on their faces, and I knew something was up. Finally, Cliff got out the video camera and hooked it to the TV. Before playing the video, he kept saying that no matter what it looks like, nobody got hurt! (It helped that I was looking at Kevin, and there were no more bumps, bruises, or scrapes than usual.)

I watched this bizarre-looking contraption go full speed down the zip line, fall apart, and crash into the mattresses designed to soften the blow at the end of the ride. Kevin was literally hanging upside down. All I saw was a helmet and what looked like his face staring at a rock. I looked at them both, shook my head, and walked away.

Yes, it was terrifying. And yes, I'm fairly certain Cliff never would have let Kevin do the zip line if he thought he would get hurt. I had to make a show of being upset and yelled a bit to make it look good. But in my heart of hearts, I was so proud of them both.

I was proud of Cliff for letting Kevin be a kid and try something fun and dangerous and for being calm in the face of what certainly looked like a horrible accident. I was proud of Kevin for being brave, fun loving, and willing to go out there and try anything. And I was proud of Kevin for letting his dad, the Scouts, and the Scout leadership have the experience of helping "that poor disabled kid" do some pretty wild and amazing stuff.

§

Every day I am thankful that we have Kevin. I am thankful for the love and joy we have despite 25 years of physical disability, pain, hospitals, surgeries, doctors, and therapies. Kevin continues to inspire us, inspire our friends, and pretty much be an amazing young man.

I'm also thankful for marrying a man who has so much love to give and continues to adapt the everyday things in our lives so that Kevin can keep going and doing—experiencing everything life has to offer.

- Bobbie Guice

24

Dear Dad: An Open Letter

Dear Dad,

Thank you for imprinting us with a love of music at a young age. I remember when Philip and I were kids, you brought us to your performances. When I was four and Philip was eight, you took us to Boston to watch you jam on the blues guitar. There are so many baby photos of Philip playing with instruments—keyboards, pianos, guitars. Philip has continued loving music into adulthood. Although with his form of autism, he has never told us this with spoken words. Philip makes it very clear that music brings him the greatest joy, next to you.

Your inspiration and guidance has led to Philip attending over twenty concerts in his life so far. He has seen some of the greatest: The Rolling Stones, The Who, Eric Clapton, Carlos Santana. He has seen more concerts than some other people his age. Philip just doesn't go along with you because he's your autistic son and he "has" to. Philip is a fellow music lover. A son and a peer. How many times has he sifted through your massive collection of CDs, tapes, and records, looking for something to play? Not only does Philip love the sound of music, he has a certain appreciation for album cover artwork. I remember him sitting by himself, flipping through your cover art compilations, glancing at a page for a minute or so, running his finger over the images.

I remember that time when Philip wandered away from home. He was only ten. We panicked, not knowing if he would find his way back or if he would get hurt. After a manhunt, you finally found him at the neighbor's, in their basement, sifting through their vinyl collection! They had called the police by then, and you explained to them that your son has a special condition and an even more special love of music.

I will never know anyone like Philip, with such an incredibly pure love of music. He is not swayed by opinions in magazines, on TV, or from musicians. He doesn't care what people think of other bands. He loves music at a level so profound that he makes everyone else look like an amateur. Though his vocabulary isn't voluminous, he can name almost every single classic rock musician playing on the classic rock radio station at any given time. Other than you, music is his favorite thing in the world.

Sometimes I think about all the times I've seen Philip and you bonding and smiling. On the couch, you and Philip will fall asleep leaning on each other's shoulders. It is a beautiful communication. You love each other so much.

Even as you got older, and Philip got bigger and had more aggressive episodes, you never stopped loving him. You bravely stood by his side and took no shame in being the father of a son with a disability. You had real pride in your son. You took what life dealt you, and you created meaning in an absurd universe. You made something beautiful out of what some would consider a tragedy.

Even when, just after an aggression by Philip, you had not just one, but two, heart attacks, and you underwent quadruple bypass surgery, your love never, ever wavered. As you started to recover, you told me that Philip gave you a reason to live. In spite of how the heart attacks affected you, you became Philip's primary caretaker and took on the responsibilities of being his personal nurse, cabbie, cook, cleaner, entertainer, and defender. I think sometimes you deserve a medal. Or maybe a Grammy?

I was so glad when you told me that you were playing music again, after years of putting it off. When you told me that you had performed at a local club and brought Philip along, I was ecstatic. We both know that music is the thing that gives Philip the greatest joy. It doesn't take much observation to see that music comforts him, gives him a feeling of safety, cheers him, and calms him down. Much the way his father does.

I believe that to enjoy music is to enjoy being alive. Music is the background in which we live our lives, helping us and healing us throughout the journey. Thank you for giving this gift to someone who can love it for what it really is. And thank you for loving Philip for who he really is.

Love always,
Natalia

- Natalia Nodiff

Dads of Disability

Transformation

We all start and end *somewhere*.

The extra transformations we are privileged to experience as a dad of disability are myriad. Don't let anyone tell you that being a dad of a child that experiences disability doesn't impact your journey—that you are selfish to say or feel that it has impacted you.

Nobody is claiming that our experiences turns devils into angels or vice-versa (though I am sure that *does* happen on occasion). We dads shouldn't place undue blame or credit on our children for our transformations.

Nevertheless, transformations *do* happen.

We are transformed by the experiences we have as dads of disability, just as we are transformed by being dads of typically developing children. Just as we are transformed by being male employees, athletes, businesspeople, artists, and on-and-on.

Disability is indeed "just part of life." And it changes those it touches.

Dads of Disability

25

The Measure of Grief

I first wrote about my son shortly after his diagnosis. His limp, bony body, the distracted doctors, the unrelenting paperwork. And, of course, our grief. But even then, I knew it wasn't writing so much as keening, a scrawled lamentation. I didn't share it with my friends, much less the public. Years passed, and I turned to less wrenching subjects. I wrote a book and various articles. I started a novel, and wrote short fiction in which stricken parents and sick children played a conspicuous role. It was as close as I could get to approaching Finn with the studied detachment that good writing requires.

Then one day in 2012, a friend asked me to write an essay for Money magazine on the financial burden of raising an autistic child. I would receive robust compensation and all the space I needed to tell a complicated story. I wish I could say I put great thought into the decision to write about my son for so large an audience, but the truth is that I don't remember it as a decision at all. I said yes because that's the learned behavior of people who write for money.

To my happy surprise, words flowed smoothly from brain to hands to page. Cursory research revealed two facts: First, that special needs children pose enormous, long-term challenges to all but the wealthiest of parents; second, my wife and I were utterly unprepared to meet those challenges. The article took on the character of a crusade. I would save thousands of families from bankruptcy and heartbreak, all while revealing the prodigious sacrifices my wife and I had made in the service of our son's disability.

In May 2013, the article, called "Paying for Finn," hit the newsstand. "Our kid is nothing like your kid," it began. "I don't mean that in an every-child-is-unique-as-a-snowflake way. I mean that my wife, Alysia, and I are pretty sure that Finn hails from some distant, unknown planet.

> His favorite foods include dirt and discarded water balloons. He spends hours a day in a headstand. He giggles maniacally at any expression of pain or distress. Recently, I caught him shattering our water glasses on the patio. While I went for the broom, he dumped a quart of milk onto our kitchen floor. I tried to scold him, but he was already engrossed in one of his favorite hobbies: smelling his right foot.

> What's wrong with this child? There are a lot of ways to answer that question. We have some acronyms, for instance: He's been diagnosed with CVI (cortical vision impairment), ASD (autism spectrum disorder), and DCD (developmental cognitive

disability). My favorite, PDD-NOS (pervasive developmental delay not otherwise specified), is the most accurate. It's doctor-speak for "We have no earthly idea what's wrong with your child."

I often find myself grasping for otherworldly metaphors to explain our experience. Imagine E.T. came to your house but never figured out how to phone home. No spaceship. No tearful departure. Just you, the other humans in the house, and E.T. He can't really communicate, so domestic dramas take place through wild gestures and improvised sign language.

"We are not of his world," Alysia and I tell ourselves. "And he is not of ours." The best we can do is help our alien child negotiate the baffling planet on which he's found himself.

My editor loved it. His boss loved it too. Alysia was proud of me and, I won't lie, I was proud, too. The piece wove our personal narrative with advice on how to set up trusts, structure investments, write wills, and otherwise tackle the peculiar aspects of providing long-term security for a special needs child. Did I want a medal? Of course not. Well, maybe, yeah. We had struggled so hard for so long, and now we were going public with our story. Accolades—or simply sympathy—just seemed like our due.

We were not disappointed. Long lost acquaintances sent emails or Facebook messages, raving about our bravery, our strength, and our honesty. "I read your article three times," one friend emailed. "Thank you so much for sharing your story so openly—I know that it's incredibly important for the world to hear it and for you to tell it." Reader emails were almost uniformly positive. There were signs, however, that not everyone saw the article in a positive light. I sent it to a friend who worked for the autism advocacy organization, Autism Speaks. I asked if he might post it to the group's Facebook page. "Sure," he said, after a halting pause. "Let me see what I can do." He didn't sound sure. Another friend close to the autism community never replied to my emails about the piece. "Hmmm," I thought. "That's unsettling." Author, meet buzzsaw.

The next week we went to Mexico for a vacation. On day three, I took my coffee out on the balcony to check my Facebook. I saw I'd been linked to a post. "Today [there] was a horribly disturbing article in a magazine about the cost of raising a special needs child," autism advocate Karla Fisher wrote on her Facebook page. If memory serves, I audibly yelped. And that was before I read the comments.

"That article made me feel sick with anger. ... That poor child has a spoiled brat for a father," wrote Tamara Rice.

"It makes me wonder whether the guy ever really wanted children in the first place," wrote Christine Hughes.

"This guy understands privilege about as well as my dog comprehends algebra," wrote Rob Gross. "What a whiny, ableist jerk."

The most hurtful were the readers who accused me of not loving my son. "Didn't anyone else find this article lacking love and warmth for the 'alien'? ... This was so cold." I had carefully—too carefully, it turns out—avoided sentiment in favor of a clear-eyed appraisal and a deadpan delivery. Alysia and I had grown to hate the saccharine treatment often afforded special needs parents and their kids. The children were always "angels," and the parents always "heroes." By contrast, I wrote, "There is no heroism in our daily life, only jury-rigged schemes, constantly changing, to help get us through each day."

And the fact is, I did, and do, love my son: "Despite it all—the broken glass, the tantrums, the bite marks, the feces Pollocked across his bedroom wall—I quite love my sweet, strange boy," I wrote further down in the article. "There are mornings when I get up early and steal into Finn's room. I drift back off to sleep, but wake to find him smiling mysteriously and running his hand over my cheek, entranced by the sensation of stubble against his inner arm. Then he giggles and tries to do a headstand on my stomach. Finn is my son, and I love him."

How could I have been more clear? At first I was outraged at the negative feedback. Many of the comments seemed to reek of condescension and an arrogance born of relative anonymity. There's a saying in the autism community: "If you've met one autistic person, you've met one autistic person." The same adage holds true for families of autistic children. How dare anyone—much less a stranger who may or may not have read the entire article—cast judgment on us, or the love I have for my son.

Friends and strangers rallied to my defense. "I'm so sorry to hear that people on the Internet are acting like people on the Internet about this," wrote a colleague. Many others came to the same conclusion: Trolls will be trolls. "Never underestimate the poor close reading skills of your average reader," noted a friend.

I was tempted to write off the critics. It would have been easy enough. But the comments kept needling me, and I found myself again and again on those blog posts or Facebook pages where my critics had gathered. I began to separate the comments written by the malicious peanut gallery from those written by people who had clearly read the article closely and responded with thoughtful commentary. Laura McKenna, a special needs parent herself, noted that I was "still firmly stuck in the grief phase of special needs parenting." Our grief over Finn's many impairments might have been "understandable," but mourning the loss of upper middle class amenities like beach vacations and a nice house was not. "Nobody is entitled to the college of their choice, a house, a fulfilling career, and a nanny," McKenna wrote. "This is selfish grief and, really, needs to end fast."

That's some bitter medicine, but I couldn't argue with the prescription. I had lived a fairly trouble-free life until my mid-30s. Then, in short order, I had to deal with nasty health issues and Finn's "global developmental delays" in the same year. Grief is a natural part of the process, I learned. Self-pity, by contrast, is corrosive. It clouds the mind's eye and weakens the soul. And the truth is that we have no cause for self-pity. We have resources most families do not enjoy. We're far from rich, but hardly poor, and we bow our heads and express gratitude for all that we have every time we sit down for dinner. Against the sacrifices made by, say, a single, unemployed mother raising a physically and mentally disabled child, my article must have smacked of privilege and, yes, self-pity.

But there was more medicine to come: "As I was reading your piece, it struck me that you were simply unaware that you were unconsciously echoing certain language that has done tremendous harm to autistic people," wrote Steve Silberman, a friend and former Wired magazine colleague currently writing a book about the history of autism and the concept of neurodiversity. "No one doubts that you love your son. But you'll be able to give his unique being the life-long support he will need more effectively if you at least try to understand where some of the criticism was coming from, rather than circling the wagons."

In writing the article, I had envisioned two sets of readers: Parents of special needs children, and everyone else. As incredible as it sounds, I had blithely—stupidly—neglected a key demographic: adults on the autism spectrum. Some of them were angry with me. Many, however, were simply hurt. Not just by me but by every neurotypical journalist like me who lapses into received wisdom and language in his or her descriptions of people like Finn as a burden to be mourned, rather than as a challenge to be managed, as we manage all the myriad hardships we happily overcome for the sake of our children. Who wants to believe that the people who should love them the most—tenderly and totally and without qualification—would publicly characterize them as a source of pain and misery?

One writer in particular brought this all home for me. "Our desire not to be rhetorically dehumanized is not a type of hatred or guilt or stone-throwing, I promise," wrote Ibby Anderson-Grace, an autistic scholar and advocate. "It is a natural reaction to hearing the type of person you are, or the type of person your kid is, talked about in ways that seem to suggest not being or counting as a human person. How do you know Finn won't read that the way you and your wife claw at each other is all his fault because he is not really a person? It isn't Finn's fault. It's insurance companies driving up costs, for one thing, and a culture of 'taxpayers' thinking there's no such thing as the good of the community and the people in it any more."

Finn read? The thought had scarcely occurred to me. Late last year we were told that Finn, in certain respects, had a "cognitive age" of an 11-month-old. We were told the same thing when Finn was two, and again when he was three, four, and five. The people doing the telling had PhDs and wore white coats and spoke warmly and a little sadly. Who were we to doubt them?

But they were wrong. Since the article came out, Finn has undergone a stunning burst of progress. He is still nonverbal, and the outward signs of his autism have hardly diminished. But he is nothing like the boy he was when the article was first published. He used to point to an object he desired. That was his one concrete method of communication. Now he uses American Sign Language gestures for music and movie and dog and shoe and food and drink and up and help and stop and wait and candy. He's beginning to shake his head no for no and nod yes for yes, and when I look into his eyes, I see now that he loves us as fiercely as we love him. He only rarely bites us anymore or wraps an angry hand around his sister's hair.

Not so long ago, I had hoped merely that some day Finn might be able to fix his own sandwich or go to the bathroom by himself. All that may well happen before his seventh birthday. How, indeed, do I know what lies in store for Finn? Will he be a composer or a writer or an engineer? Or simply a human just like the rest of us, full of abilities and disabilities both, as well as the welter of emotions that afflict our strange species. I've come to see that the very things that differentiate him from a neurotypical child are his most charming attributes. While he may not speak, he does purr, and he makes a bewildering array of dolphin clicks that can only be expressive in nature. I've become so accustomed to his hand-flapping exhilaration that I'm amazed all humans don't employ the gesture to communicate joy. Do I want to "cure" my son? It would be like sending E.T. home. And we quite like having him here with us on this foreign planet, the culture clash notwithstanding.

And yet, despite all this, I cannot avoid the lexicon of illness. Last spring he escaped the gate we constructed around our yard and wandered three blocks to his favorite grocery store. Like any parents, we were frantic with fear and worry until the police informed us that he was in their somewhat confused custody. Unlike other parents, we felt a very unique terror. Does Finn understand what a road is? A car? Quite possibly not. The previous month he had climbed out of his bedroom window, falling two-and-a-half stories, breaking his pelvis and fracturing two vertebrae. I can love Finn for his Finn-ness. But I cannot avoid words like "impaired" or "delayed" or "nonverbal," or the phrase that particularly irks so many autism advocates, "low functioning." Finn is still in diapers. The ability to defecate in a socially responsible manner would fall, surely, under the most basic of functions.

A vocal subset of ASD adults has opened a schism in a community already starved for resources. They charge Autism Speaks, the leading advocacy organization, with treating autism as a disease to be cured. To the quirky Intel programmer recently diagnosed with Asperger's, that surely seems like a personal affront. To people struggling to raise a child incapable of communication, toileting, or controlling a physically violent temper, pathologizing autism isn't much of a reach. It's ironic, and a little tragic, to see an increasingly angry war of words erupt within a community in such desperate need of unity.

Not everyone is ready to man the battlements: "Some of the people who most fervently believe families should have help and support are also disabled," notes Anderson-Grace. "We could be natural allies and help each other mobilize for action. This is a thing I personally want to see happen with great passion, and work for often." Let that work begin.

- Jeff Howe

26

Labels

Before I became a dad, I never gave a second thought to labeling people. In fact, I am sure I was a "jump-to-conclusions, people-labeling" offender. How things change with the birth of one little girl.

The only labels I wanted for our little girl Megan were words like "angel," "sweetie," or even "daddy's little girl." Having a daughter instantly brought out my fatherly instincts, which of course included keeping her safe. This genetic imperative we dads have makes the world of labels challenging.

Megan entered our lives in 1995 and was later given a chromosomal diagnosis of Isodicentric 15. Her first label wasn't even understandable by 98% of the population! But I was okay with it because at least it gave us a name for and a reason to attach to her lack of typical accomplishments or milestones. Also, it was not an offensive label, and it did not hamper my instincts as a dad to shield my daughter from the world.

As Megan entered the school system, the evaluations that took place always looked to put labels on our daughter. I was very hesitant at first, but I quickly learned that labels are used as gatekeepers. By asking her doctor to add a secondary diagnosis (and label) of autism, something we didn't want at first, Megan now had access to a wider range of services that she needed. Ironically, her rare primary chromosomal diagnosis would not have allowed her access to these services. On the whole, this was good for Megan, and I accepted the additional label.

But not all labels are acceptable. Before Megan's birth and the softening effect of having a daughter with a disability, I would use crude language to describe people I did not understand. Perhaps you've done it, too. Have you ever see an individual walking down the street in an awkward manner or maybe holding on someone's arm, who doesn't seem quite "right?" Before, I was quick to say, "Look at that retarded person," and would even joke about it.

Now the mere mention of that word, even in jest, makes my skin crawl and my whole being cringe. It reminds me of a time when Megan was around four and I was still very fragile and inexperienced in this world of special needs. I was at work, and we had a computer training class. We had just come back from a short break and were all gathered around a computer screen. One of the attendees started talking about an error that someone had made on the production floor. He was very detailed and started using the word "retarded" to describe the error. The first time he said it, I cringed internally. But then he used it again and again.

At this point, as a dad with a daughter with a disability, my natural instincts to protect and fight back kicked in. I asked him to stop using that language to describe the error as it was offensive to me and my daughter. He looked at me in disbelief and was ready to dismiss my comment and continue his rudeness. Since I was already at a computer station, I quickly navigated to the web page that had my daughter's diagnosis published on it. Under the description of her story was the list of symptoms and traits. There it was in black and white. One of the characteristics of the disorder was even referred to as "retardation." Obviously the individual felt bad at that point and might even think twice about using that language in the future, but it definitely ended that particular use of the word on that day.

I will admit that was a strong approach and arguably an immature one, no matter how right it seemed. At that point, I was new to it all and would definitely handle it better now that I am a well-seasoned dad. Maybe it was just a dad thing, protecting our children from the cruel world of labels.

I understand that for some, "retardation" is still an acceptable medical term and has technical meaning, but it is a very crude and inaccurate label. Having Megan in our lives has made me very open minded and sympathetic to any individual that appears to be impaired in one way or another. We all have a story, and unless I know that person's story, it is not my place to judge or label

Another label screams out at us daily from the parking lot: The "Handicapped" spot. As a teenager, I would not hesitate to pull into one of those spots if I was in a hurry to run in and out of a store. I had no regard or respect for the sign and functionality of the spot for people who really did need it.

How much change can happen to a person's thinking when you are exposed to and immersed in the world of disabilities. I have now become a handicapped parking spot advocate. I am very conscious of these spots and find myself looking to make sure I actually see a handicapped plate or hanging placard on the vehicle.

I remember one time when Megan was about eight, we had decided to go to the movies as a family. With all five of us sitting the car, I arrived at the theater parking lot and remember circling looking for a closer parking spot. There were none to be found. However, I did note that a car with a couple of people in it had parked in a handicapped spot but were obviously just waiting for someone to come out. There was no plate or placard visible. We ended up parking in the far corner of the lot, taking everyone out, and starting our trek across the parking lot.

Without warning, I passed my daughter over to my wife to continue guiding her in with the other kids. I walked over to the parked car and asked the person to lower the window. When they did, I pointed out my wife and daughter walking across the lot. I told them that if they had respected the parking spot, I could have parked in a convenient location for my daughter who actually needed it versus using it as an easy location to pick someone up. Again, this is a bit extreme, nor do I advocate doing this, but as a guy, as a dad, and as a dad of a little girl with special needs, I felt moved to action.

You would think as a parent of a child with a disability, we might be immune to the crudeness of labels. But this is not the case for me. This is our child. We will do whatever it takes to raise her in a way that makes her happy. Sometimes that includes labeling her, and other times it includes being sensitive to, or even objecting to, labels.

Fighting the label battle over time is hard. But that battle, like many others a father faces while raising a child with severe special needs, is small compared with the reward. When Megan lays her head on the pillow at the end of the day and requests her good night kiss ("Kiss-kiss," she says.), all the labels in the world melt away except for one: *daughter.*

- Paul Rivard

Dads of Disability

27

Take Me Out to the Ballgame

As a guy, you know intrinsically that at a minimum, you need to provide three basics for yourself and your family: clothing, shelter, and food. These are the evolutionary mandates that lay the groundwork for a fulfilling life. It all seems pretty straightforward until a wrench gets thrown into any of these "big three."

For my family, food became the basis for upending those basic tenants. For the outsider, it would be easy to say (as many have), "Oh you just have a food issue. It shouldn't be that hard, right?" These words echo in my head every time I find myself explaining my son's circumstances to new people. Often they equate my son's issue with a food allergy like peanuts or strawberries. I wish it was that simple.

Our son Parker has Phenylketonuria, or PKU for short. PKU is a rare genetic condition in which the body cannot break down the essential amino acid phenylalanine, which is present at some level in a majority of foods. Phenylalanine levels are drastically higher in anything that has protein or artificial sweeteners. If PKU is managed correctly, there are no real outward signs that anything is amiss. It's an invisible disability. But without diagnosis and management, phenylalanine builds up in the system and causes permanent nervous system and brain damage. If ignored, there can be issues, such as severe intellectual disability, seizures, tremors, hyperactivity, stunted growth, and eczema, and a musty odor often thought to be something else.

PKU isn't a trendy disorder. It certainly doesn't garner the headline-grabbing attention of autism, spina bifida, cerebral palsy, and other issues. Most people have never even heard of PKU. And that's ironic, considering that the heel-prick test their child received at birth tested for PKU and other rare disorders. It impacts 1 in every 10-15,000 live births. Nor does PKU have massive amounts of funding and research dedicated to finding a cure or viable treatment. Drug companies have little incentive to spend the money on medicine for a really small number of people.

PKU isn't a food allergy. In contrast, food allergies' impacts are usually visible, are often outgrown, and while effectively dealing with allergies is certainly no small feat, they quite often are treated by just avoiding a very small and very particular type of food. With PKU, the consequences of phenylalanine buildup are not outwardly apparent at first. It has a cumulative effect, is irreversible, and you never outgrow it. And phenylalanine is present in almost all foods.

Especially "manly" foods.

This was a mountain to climb for me as a guy and a dad who grew up in a culture where food was extremely important to the men in the family. We ate—often and a lot. Although my Italian mother did most of the actual cooking, it was my Slovak father's influence on food that I most identified with. She cooked what he wanted to eat, and we ate it whether we liked it or not.

My paternal grandmother owned a restaurant and was a caterer. Man, could she cook. There was always food on the stove and always what my dad liked to eat. She also had a big family that often held guy-centric events, like football, baseball, fishing, and hunting, that were always focused on food. Even when we went out to eat with the family, we went where my dad or the men of the family wanted to go. It wasn't so much what you ate or what was made but that there was always lots to choose from. All delicious and all centered on what the guys wanted to eat: barbecued ribs, steak, pork anything, and sausage-stuffed cabbage rolls, an unending parade of meat-centric delicacies.

When we found out I was going to become a father, I was excited to pass this tradition along. Then, when we found out about Parker's diagnosis, it was like getting punched in the gut. I found myself, like so many others, trying to convince myself and my wife that this was no big deal. "Oh it's just a food issue. That shouldn't be hard, right?" (Sound familiar?). My world was turned upside down. All of a sudden, something that was culturally essential to me as a man, the experience of great food, that I wanted so excitedly to share with my son was no longer going to happen. Ever.

Regardless, I did what any loving and dedicated father would do to help their child. I got educated, found resources, and joined a support group. We were fortunate that we lived in a state where the insurance companies were required to pay not only for his care but for the metabolic formula and low-protein food that has become the source of nourishment he could not live without. The formula is a powder, much like baby formula, where the processing has already converted the phenylalanine his body can't. We reconstitute it, and Parker drinks it. The formula is a complete nutrition, just lacking in one simple thing—enough calories to sustain him.

Here is where my challenge started. For the first time in my adult male life, I had to actually think about food in a very different way. It was a foreign concept to me. Guys just eat. We don't think about calories, protein content, or spend our time looking for artificial sweetener (in our case, to avoid it at all costs). Wasn't that an activity that people did to watch their weight?

I felt guilty thinking about Parker growing up with me munching on a cheeseburger while he had to drink formula and eat apples and carrot sticks. Would he want what I had? How could he resist the smell of barbecued ribs or hamburgers on the grill, or worse yet, one of my favorite food groups, homemade pizza? His uncle is a chef and makes fantastic ribs, steaks, and burgers. Would he never be able to enjoy the male bonding over food that I experience? How could I figure out what to feed him that didn't look like I pulled it out of the lawn mower? Would there be enough for him to eat at all, and how would he cook it?

Unfortunately, we now live in a place where neither the insurance company nor the state pays for his food, which is extremely expensive. For example, a 16 oz box of low-protein pasta costs 5 to 6 times what standard pasta costs because it is only made overseas. If you have any items requiring refrigeration during shipping (cold ship items), there is a minimum order, so you sometimes have to go without or order more than you really need and hope you can afford it. It is close to impossible to get basic food items for Parker that typical eaters wouldn't think twice about running to the local market to get on a whim. I have a decent job and earn a good living, but our insurance is not great. His medical expenses plus the food can really add up fast. The economics could crush a family with lesser means facing the same challenges. I don't know how they do it. We decided to only have one child because the financial impact of possibly having two with the disorder was beyond our means. Yet there are many families that do have multiple kids with PKU and have to bear those expenses.

Our world now revolves around food but in a very different way than I had anticipated or longed for. As Parker has been growing, we have been diligent about weighing and measuring everything, writing everything down, getting the necessary blood tests, and teaching him about what he can and can't have and how much. I sound like a broken record when I have to tell him that just because it is low protein doesn't mean it's no protein. He has been good for the most part so far in parroting back to people saying, "I can't have that because I have PKU" or grabbing safe snacks like sugar candy or an apple.

He knows he's different, and we try to get him to understand that everyone has different challenges. But you can see the disappointment in his eyes when a parent surprises the class with ice cream, or he's is at a birthday party and can't have the cake, only the sugar frosting. He has watched his friends and classmates at the cafeteria pick what they want while he is relegated to his packed lunch of cucumber slices, applesauce, and low-protein bread. The conversations are getting harder as he gets older.

Now he is ten years old. I do the majority of cooking in my house for dinner, and pizza is still on the menu as are plenty of meat dishes. I make his low-to-no-protein dinner alongside ours, but since he is so active (he also has ADHD), he generally is done before my wife and I even sit to eat. So Parker isn't usually forced to watch me eat a steak or hamburger or tacos. However, he does smell the food I cook and looks at the skillet with wonder. He often asks for a pinch of pizza crust because it tastes better than his. It gets harder to hold the line.

Home is safe and easy. We can control the environment. Traveling or eating out is a whole other level of crazy. You have to bring your kitchen with you no matter where you go and study the restaurant menu to see if there is any shred of sustenance he can have. The food we bring with us doesn't reheat well, especially in a commercial microwave, and often doesn't keep, so there can be a lot of waste. If it goes bad or turns hard, you are out of luck and wind up with a sobbing, hungry child with nothing to feed him until you get home. Parker is a kid and fickle, so if all of a sudden he doesn't want what you brought, it isn't like you can just grab something else.

Parker is learning portions but hasn't quite gotten it. Wait staff can be accommodating but don't understand that when you say that he can have some French fries, you are not thinking about a five-pound basket of fries, only to have him shriek when you have to remove most of the fries from his plate. (A typical restaurant portion of fries contains his protein allowance for the entire week.)

Flying anywhere or going long distances presents a bigger challenge. You have to make sure you have enough formula for the trip and then some, in case you get stuck somewhere. You don't dare put it in checked luggage lest it get lost in transit. That creates inquisitive looks and queries from the TSA about several cans of white powder with no infant in sight.

I most recently experienced dramatic impact when we went to a baseball game together. It started as the best father-son moment: warm summer's day with just me and my son sitting in the lower deck behind home plate watching our team play America's favorite pastime. I had brought a cooler with me with some safe foods and knew I could splurge on a small fries we could share from the concessions stand. He was excited to be there sitting on the edge of his seat rooting for our team.

During the seventh-inning stretch, an elderly man sitting right behind us leaned over and commented on how it was nice to see a young man so engaged in the game and how polite he was. Then it happened. He thought he was doing a nice thing for us. I was too involved in my son's excitement in the game to notice what the man was up to. Otherwise, I would have stopped him. It was a simple, thoughtful gesture. The gentleman bought him some peanuts and a hot dog from one of the vendors. As I have taught him before, he turned to the man and said thank you but he couldn't have it because he had PKU, as if that explained everything. I was proud of my son for being polite.

The puzzled look on the man's face said it all. He looked at me as if I thought he was offering poison to my son. How right he was (if that is what he was thinking). I said thank you again, offered to pay him back, and told him my son couldn't eat the food because of a metabolic disorder. I tried to give the Cliffs Notes version of PKU and protein. He kindly asked if that was some sort of food allergy, and rather than give him the medical detail, I simply said yes. Parker's face got red, and he looked at the ground the rest of the game until we left at the middle of the ninth inning. He was no longer enjoying the game.

It wasn't until we were driving home listening to the final at bat that he said to me, "I wish I didn't have PKU, so I could have eaten that food. It smelled good." I offered him some of the food left in the cooler, an apple sauce cup and some fruit chews, but he just got quiet, and I got sad. I was sad because here was a simple situation that is played out between guys and their sons at ball parks across America: Watching a game and eating hot dogs and peanuts.

I knew then that he was starting to realize what he can't have rather than what he can. I will never share that part of the game with him. So I tried to focus on the game itself and the fact that we shared that as father and son, but it still came back to the food. As he comes of age, I'm in the process of learning it is not about me as a dad; it is about him as a son. If I was to share with him that bonding experience, it had to be on his terms, not mine. It wasn't going to get easier as he enters his tweens and teens. But I needed to bond on his terms. He said he was hungry but didn't want the snacks in the cooler. I knew he was thinking about the hot dog and peanuts.

We have been warned by his nutritionist and others with older kids with PKU that the teen years are the hardest. The kids want to sneak food or go off the prescribed dietary treatment, often with less-than-desirable or even catastrophic results. They will be tempted by peer pressure to eat things they shouldn't or in quantities that will equate to a week's "normal" protein intake, like a cheeseburger. They will get angrier, depressed, and rebel like all teens do.

I hope I have instilled the right attitude and the tools to arm my child to make the better choice for his health and how to deal with people who might not get it. Medical advances happen all the time for many of the major disorders and occasionally, even for people with PKU. We will always hope that one day there will be a cure or treatment that significantly relaxes the diet or provides enzymatic activity secure enough to allow him to eat what he wants.

I have learned from him to think about what I put in my own mouth. And to search for things we can bond over as father and son that he chooses. And, hopefully, he continues to think of what he has learned, so we can continue to share good moments around food.

And even take in a ball game or two.

- Raymond Kent

Dads of Disability

28

What Does His Mother Think?

Without circumstances warranting it, a father should never be viewed as a secondary caregiver—or less. At a minimum, the father should be considered a peer of the mother. Sometimes, the father is more of a caregiver than the mother. Yet even in 2014, it is hard for some to see the latter as a possibility.

I was married to my first wife for 18 years, during which time we had two children: a boy born in 1980 and a daughter four years later. My wife was the primary parent for the years that preceded school. But when my daughter started school, we decided that my wife would follow a career path and that I (being self-employed in design work) had the flexibility to be at home more for the children. Over the years, I took on more of the child rearing responsibilities: I became the one in closest contact with my children's schools and doctors and generally tended to their education, well being, and socialization. I was what we think of as "the modern father." I loved that time with my children and wouldn't have changed a thing.

Both of our children were bright, well socialized, popular, and very happy. As a parent, I really had it easy!

Then, when my son reached the age of 17, the unexpected happened. Previously an extremely outgoing and popular lad, my son began to withdraw from others. His schoolwork started to fail. Inexplicably, he slowly fell into a deep depression. No amount of understanding or encouragements or chastisements or freedoms seemed to pull him out of this. Doctors were reluctant to give advice to me about a patient who refused to visit them or accept that he was depressed. My son was just old enough by now to be considered autonomous, and by law, his health was his business. I could not convince him of the need to see a doctor of any kind despite agreement from his school and doctor that help was clearly needed.

It was very difficult to watch.

After almost a year of slow deterioration, my son suddenly developed psychotic behavior. He became alarmingly and psychologically ill. He was diagnosed with schizophrenia that was both severe and would prove long lasting. Within a few months of the official schizophrenia diagnosis, I barely recognized him. He looked like my son, he sounded like my son, but his personality was that of someone else. He was no longer "socially able" and has remained disabled ever since. I visited him in the psychiatric ward of the local hospital and spent time with him there. But he seemed absent. Although I was with him, he seemed to be lost within himself.

I fell into a mourning that lasted for many years. I felt that this disability had robbed me of my son, and robbed my son of a meaningful life.

Suddenly, I was the father of a severely disabled child and had no idea how to best deal with this, or how I might be able to offer anything loving and useful to his life. I would visit him often, occasionally having him stay with me overnight or through weekends, when his psychiatric consultants agreed that would be beneficial. I found myself floundering in unknown territory.

Very quickly, I learned that a father of a disabled child of any age has to overcome some difficulties that are very specific to fathers. Prior to my son's diagnosis, my wife and I had separated, and we were in the process of divorce, so I was doing much on my own.

Society, in general, still assumes that a father's job is to take care of the mechanical upbringing of children. They assume that the father offers a stable, financially secure income, that he is responsible for punishments and rewards, and that he leads by good example. It is assumed that the relationship between a father and son is less likely to be overtly loving or physically close. In the United Kingdom (where I was born and lived at the time), one rarely hugs one's son, particularly when they are older. The English do not expect to show open displays of affection between a father and son.

I was saddened to discover that it was not assumed that fathers have the emotional resources to take on the responsibilities that mothers are more commonly expected to fulfill. When visiting my son in hospital and attending social worker meetings, I was aware that the burning questions were usually centered around my son's mother: "What does his mother think? What does his mother say? Is his mother OK with that? Would his mother agree?" My ex-wife did all she could to help, but emotionally she was not as clued in to our son as I was. Practically speaking, though she loved him deeply, she knew him less well than I did. But, as a father, I was seen by the extended team as merely someone who just "helped." I was not seen as a primary caregiver, but a secondary one or worse, an irrelevant one. For quite a while, I would even say I was treated as a nuisance by the psychiatric consultants and welfare representatives.

It didn't seem to make any difference that I was the person they needed to come to for information about my son's school, his doctor, how he spent most of his time in the past, what he might respond to, and what kind of approach may not work well for him. I knew my son better than anyone in the world could have and cared for him as well as any father could, but still I was always a helper not a primary caregiver in the eyes of professionals.

It took many years for the veils to fall from the eyes of the professionals who were in direct counseling with my son. I experienced blank stares from those in the medical and welfare system, and heard the inevitable, "Yes, but what does his mother say?" far too many times for far too long. Eventually, notes in psychiatrists' notebooks did somehow get through to consultant after consultant, and I was made the official primary caregiver of my son. Dialog with consultants, social workers, and the social services then became easier and more fruitful, even though I was the same father that I always had been.

While I have been successful in overcoming this prejudice in my situation, too many involved and active fathers of children with disabilities continue to be dismissed as nonessential. These fathers are not merely helpers but are peer, if not primary, caregivers. They deserve to be heard and acknowledged within the medical system and by society as a whole. One day, I hope a father's love, sense of responsibility, and significant role in child rearing will be seen as the norm, rather than the exception—recognized and celebrated!

- Paul Digby

Dads of Disability

29

Playing with Blueberries and Cream

For the last few months, my young daughter has been meeting with an occupational therapist (OT) to help with her sensory issues. Our new OT has Grace play with quinoa because she refuses to put her feet down on sand. He gets her hands sticky and tries to distract her cries to wash them. He gets her shirt wet and tries to distract her cries to change.

I didn't realize I had sensory issues until I learned about my daughter's. Then it made sense why I hate turtlenecks, or why I freak out if my clothes stain or when I feel constricted or constrained. I didn't realize my issues weren't just a problematic personality.

When we were first learning that Grace wouldn't eat spongy foods, or didn't like kids her age (too unpredictable), or couldn't stand clothes too tight on her arms, my mom would sometimes say something like, "That's how Matthew was." And I would learn about my genetic handicaps from things I had forgotten about myself.

I remember I used to have desperate fights with my father over mowing the lawn. I remember it felt like I was being dropped in acid when the grass would shoot up from the blades and touch my skin. I couldn't breathe and used to run away from home over this. I fought until my parents must have thought I was crazy. If only we had known these were sensory issues. I couldn't explain what was wrong.

They thought I had a behavioral problem.

The things parents learn over generations.

Today, the OT had us buy whipped cream and blueberries. I have stayed home for the day to drive to the grocery store and now to help out. The OT sprays the cream on a paper plate and drops the blueberries in it with tiny foamy splashes. Grace watches. He asks her to pick them out of it. He asks her to decorate her plastic cake. He asks her to sort the blue from the white.

At first, this is all fun and games. Then the cream dries into a layer of film. It gets on Grace's clothes. It clings to her hands. When she whimpers, when she begs, it breaks my heart. She holds her little palms out to us. The OT makes this moaning sound and says, "Uh oh," and claps at her like a dog. The OT says we should put our hands in to show her it is okay.

Cathreen puts her hands in, so I have to put in mine. I have to keep my face looking happy, encouraging, but the feeling of the cream makes me want to run. The only reason I do not is that I am doing this for my daughter. The embarrassment alone would not stop me now. Looking like a scared toddler would be an easy trade for clean hands, if I didn't have a scared toddler of my own.

"See," Cathreen says. "It's okay."

"See," I say. "It's okay."

Grace plays a little longer, then cries more. It is all I can do to sit still now. Something crawls up the insides of my ribs. I can't even encourage her. I can only keep my face from mirroring hers.

The layer of dried cream is like I'm wearing a dead person's skin as gloves.

Finally, Grace can't take anymore, and the OT lets us get the baby wipes. I try not to grab at them. As soon as I can, I make a break for the kitchen.

I hear my daughter rallying in the other room, doing better than I am. I wash once, twice. I smell my hands. They still smell like cream, and just the smell brings on dizziness.

I can feel tears, unstoppable now. I can't manage this mess. I haven't cried like this, without being sad (or knowing why I'm sad?), in years. I try to think whether there might be some memory, or trauma, connected to this feeling, but I don't get anywhere. Soon I am crouched down in a ball, weeping as silently as I can.

When the OT comes out, I quickly stand and wipe my eyes. He says what a good job Grace did. I try to get him to leave.

When Cathreen comes out, I tell her what happened. I tell her I had zero control over my reactions. I am opening and closing my hands into fists. My palms feel like deserts.

"That is why we doing this," she says. "We don't want her to become you."

The awkward phrasing stings, but I understand what she means. My genes. My fault.

No, we don't want Grace to become me. We want her to become something far better: herself. We will have failed as parents if she doesn't improve on us generationally.

We want our daughter to grow out of her sensory problems, or at least understand them if they still exist later. We want her to know she is understood. We want her to know when to push herself or refuse to push. We want her to learn who she is, to discover each day a little more of what might even be a mystery to us.

- Matthew Salesses

A version of this essay previously appeared in *The Good Men Project*.

30

Boxes in the Night

One evening my wife and I were awakened to the terrified cries of our seven-year-old son downstairs. Hyrum did not really begin speaking until he was about five. That's when his little sister started catching up with and surpassing his level of speech. At age seven, his speech was still delayed and not always intelligible. That's why this particular night we were surprised to hear him speaking fluently. He was speaking in short sentences, very coherently. He repeated, "Please bring my boxes back from the landfill. Don't let the trash compactor eat them!" Over and over again he repeated these sentences, with tears streaming down his face.

The boxes he referred to were bicycle boxes I had stored behind our garage. At the time, I was running a small bicycle shop and had stashed about 20 large bicycle boxes in the backyard where Hyrum had played with them over the summer. One day it rained long and hard and ruined the boxes, so I had to get rid of them.

I was surprised at Hyrum's meltdown because he was there when I threw the boxes out a few months ago. He never seemed to grieve for them before. But here it was on a cold rainy night in the fall at 11 p.m., and he was realizing just how much he missed those bicycle boxes. To him it was a tragedy of great importance. He needed to have them back.

My mind was racing. What could have triggered this panic? Was it a random nightmare? Maybe he had recently seen a box outside? Maybe it was from watching "The Brave little Toaster?" That might explain why he was worried about the boxes getting eaten by the trash compactor. Whatever had triggered Hyrum, I knew I had to do something.

The super hero inside of me thought, "I have some new bike boxes in the garage. Maybe I could pull out a few and make him believe I had brought them back! We could have the ultimate adventure and sleep outside in the rain with a few blankets and two of those boxes on top of us! Yes, that would make him happy!" I was in my underwear. I didn't know where my glasses were. But dang it, I was going to grab a flashlight and jacket and trip over the junk in the shed if I had to. Just to find those boxes and make this right. Exasperation, sleep deprivation, and the meltdown of a young child with autism often makes champions of us all.

About the time I snapped out of this fast-paced hero fantasy, I saw my wife holding Hyrum in her arms. She was rocking him to sleep and drying his tears. He whimpered and sobbed for a few minutes. He finally passed out, peaceful in his mother's arms. As his breathing calmed down and my wife rocked him, I flashed back to memories of my own mother.

One day when I was a child, we returned from school to find out that Mom had donated most of our stuffed animals to the local thrift store. Our beloved stuffed animals: Racoony, Dolphinny, and Humphrey the gorilla! You would have thought the world had ended. We cried and cried. When Mom realized the severity of her crime, she did the best she could to console us. She was even ready to take us back to the thrift store to go and find them for us.

As my wife continued to rock Hyrum, a thousand more memories flew by of my mom picking me up after falling off my bike, helping us bury our dead guinea pigs in the garden, and plopping her scoop of mint ice cream in my empty cone after my scoop of bubble gum ice cream fell on the hot asphalt. Moms have a way to make things right.

But dads can do a pretty good job, too! I remember my dad coming to our terrible violin concerts and always telling us he was proud of us. I remember Dad volunteering at a high adventure camp sacrificing his vacation to be with his boys. I remember him sticking up for me when I had a pony tail in high school.

Yes, even dads can make things better.

As it turned out, that night I didn't get to play superhero. My wife put Hyrum back in his bed, and there was no mention of the boxes again for some time. Though I did keep a couple of boxes on hand, just in case. Like all good fathers, I would gladly rush out in the middle of the night to pick up an empty bicycle box in the rain if it meant I could console my child. When a child cries out in the night, "Dad, I need you!" it doesn't matter if the child has a disability or not. You are Dad. Just Dad. Sometimes the disability label and non-standard reality make you forget that.

You are just Dad.

Remember, the next time you are frustrated and tempted to be embarrassed because your child is having a meltdown on aisle 17. Or your child messed themselves in public with no bathroom in sight. Or you accidentally snag your child's oxygen line or G-tube as you pull them out of the car seat. No matter how much it feels like the world is watching and judging you—or if people are *really* judging you out loud—remember that what matters most is that your child knows you love them, and you are there for them in the best way you know how.

Buy that extra ice cream cone, find that lost toy, be that hero. Give your children the atypical attention or support that they need, even if the world judges you based on a reality that isn't yours. After all, it's nobody's business why you keep old, folded bicycle boxes in the back of the hall closet.

- Rusty Earl

31

Running Away

I can hear her breathing. Why do I fear her so much? She is my own flesh and blood, yet I lie silently in my bed hoping she will not be here in the morning. What kind of father am I? What kind of father secretly prays that his daughter will quietly disappear in the middle of the night instead of facing another day with her?

For two weeks I prayed for God to heal her, but of course, he did not grant my desperate request. What kind of God would allow my daughter to suffer when I offered my own life and salvation to heal her? These Down syndrome parents I read about are only tricking themselves into thinking their child is normal. All of my friends have normal children they can watch grow and develop, but not us. Is this your idea of fairness, God? Supposedly you are a just God, but after dedicating seven years to serving you in Thailand, I lay here listening to this human I created and know she will never succeed in this world.

Why is Marley the daughter you chose to put in my life? I have already failed her, my wife, and myself. Just twelve months ago, my life was completely different. Now

I hate this extra chromosome I can't see, I hate my wife for helping me create this child, I hate You for not answering my prayers, and I hate myself for having to live this unchangeable situation until the day I die. In fact, God, how about you let me die tonight to escape this pain that has overcome my every waking moment? I can hear her raspy up-and-down breathing. I am a worthless excuse for a father, and I truly believe my wife and child would be better off without me. Selfishly, I don't want this life, but truthfully, I am disgusted by the pathetic title I now carry as a father. What kind of father is suddenly fearful of his own child because of two words said by a doctor? "Down syndrome."

You took my father when I was eighteen, and now you are taking the dreams I had for my only little girl.

§

He was my catcher and I was his pitcher. By my junior year, I was throwing in the mid-eighties, but my dad would still catch me with nothing on but a glove. We would throw for hours in the yard as he would squat and catch me. This might not seem like a great feat, but he was already over 50 by my senior year of high school. He was the most honest catcher I have ever worked with, but I could not be honest with him on that last day of catch.

I still believe the only reason he wanted to play catch was to prove to me he could overcome cancer. Why else would a guy be in the yard playing catch after having a brain tumor removed a few months earlier? I started by just softly tossing the ball, and he quickly became angry. "Stop babying it," he said. After a few more minutes, I stared letting the ball go, and the first true fastball I threw whistled by his ear and hit the car. He wanted to keep going. I was on the verge of tears, but I was taught when your dad tells you to do something, you do it. He told me to throw a curve, so he could see how my breaking stuff was looking. When I threw the ball, it short hopped him and hit him in the face. He put his glove down and looked up at me with his swollen eye. The pain I saw in his face was not a physical hurt, but the fear of a man that had been defeated. I knew at that moment that things would never be the same, and I was losing my father. After that event, we talked very little, and he slowly lost a battle that I always thought he would win.

I sat and watched my father die while trying to juggle baseball, college, and a girlfriend. I did what I believed most boys would do when a father becomes terminal: I ran. The pain of watching a man deteriorate to not walking, not talking, and not moving was more than I could handle at eighteen. A man that could beat me in a 40-yard dash just a few years earlier had wasted away to less than a 100 pounds in 12 months.

I started drinking heavily and spending nights at my girlfriend's house in another town. I smoked pot and avoided my family at all costs. I dropped out of college and hated baseball. I knew my dad was dying, and all I wanted was to numb the pain. I think we are equipped as humans to handle suffering and pain, but there comes a point were our body shuts down because it is too much to bear. I reached that point on April 12th, 1998, when my dad died. Everything we had worked for was gone. Nothing seemed to matter after he was lowered into a grave.

Most boys will endure the death (physically or emotionally) of a father at some point in their lives. Odds are we will watch them leave our lives in some way before our own death. I believe when that happens, a small part of us dies with them. Everyone debates why many of the sons of our generation become absent fathers in adulthood. The answer has always been simple for me: When a boy loses—or worse, never has—a father, he misses out on something that no other person can ever completely replace. And that has an impact on a boy and a man.

§

I do believe that God plays a significant role in my life, but I think the foundation of every boy's story should start with a different character: dad. If the relationship with our earthly father is damaged, certain pieces of our relationship with our eternal Father might be broken. This might be difficult for many to accept because a father might have never been present in your life. But I would argue that at the time any child loses his father, he or she immediately loses an irreplaceable presence in his or her life. The loss might occur before birth or in the golden years, but regardless of how worthless a father might seem, he is still significant to that child. When the man that carries the title of father is absent, the child will always suffer, regardless of age.

§

Some people may believe my father was too hard on me. I remember getting hurt playing pick-up basketball on a Friday night after my dad had told me not to play because we had an important baseball game on Saturday. I rolled my ankle pretty badly, and that night I was icing it when I heard my parents fighting downstairs. My father was adamant I was going to play because it was my responsibility to the team. My mom was telling him that he was crazy, and I could hurt my ankle more. As I was lying there listening to them argue, I knew he would make me play because he believed in loyalty. I have met very few veterans, as my dad was, that did not value loyalty over most other things.

The next day I played and remember hobbling around the field. The dramatic play where I had a chance to be a hero was late in the game. I was on second base when the guy on my team got a base hit to center field. I rounded third and looked at the coach, my father, giving me the stop signal. I didn't care, I was going to be the hero and prove my father wrong. I sprinted home and slid into the catcher as he caught the ball and tagged me. I looked up at the umpire and he yelled, "Out!"

When the umpire called me out I began to cry, and everyone thought I was hurt. I grabbed my knee and started rolling around on the ground. My father came down the baseline from third and told me to get up. The umpire told him he thought I was seriously hurt, and I remember another one of those famous father lines "He is not physically hurt, his feelings are hurt because he got tagged out at home. So get up." I then felt him jerk me up and drag me back to the dugout. I heard a gasp though the crowd as I was hobbling back to the dugout with my father dragging me along. He whispered to me in that moment, "I thought your ankle was hurt not your knee? If you don't start walking, you are going to get it when we get home." I knew that meant the switch (a tree branch used for discipline), so I stopped hobbling and reluctantly walked with him back to the dugout. We lost the game, and the switch was waiting on me when we got home.

In today's world, my father might be going in front of a judge to discuss child abuse, but except for the choice of discipline, he was right. I had lost the game and decided to fake the severity of my injury when the umpire called me out. My mother would have coddled me if my father were not present on that day. That probably would have led me down a path of more whining and excuse making in my future years. Sometimes no one else can see the truth except for your dad.

§

The dynamic duo of a mother and a father is important for a reason. A child needs the balance of a caring father and caring mother. When this influential family model is broken, the child is going to suffer. The traditional family is a necessity for our children. Fathers who leave their children are already taking away a relationship that can never be replaced by anyone else. My father is the reason I am the man I am today.

Without his guidance, I know I would have left my child, my wife, and my faith. The model of loyalty I witnessed in him for 18 years challenged me to work through my own fear and inadequacies, and be a father for my daughter. Until fathers accept the vital importance of raising their children, we are going to have broken children in this world who never understand the true value of having a dad.

§

I am a father now. Marley has completely changed my life. How I long to talk to my father about being a father! I try to talk to other fathers, but it is not the same as being able to talk to my own. My dad was a deeply religious man, and church was the only place we spent as much time as a baseball field. He was strict and believed hard work could accomplish anything. (I realize he was not perfect, and there are things I hope to change in using him as my role model. But imperfection is an important lesson, too!)

At age 34, I often think back to my father's guidance when I encounter difficult situations. I think about how he never questioned God, regardless of the circumstances. Or how he would pick up the mentally-challenged man in our town and give him a ride anywhere he wanted to go. It did not matter what our plans were at that moment. If someone needed a ride, we would take him. My father was a unique person, and he was always there willing to help me with life. Even though my father never met my daughter, I know what his advice would be in raising Marley:

> *"Well, she has Down syndrome. So what? Look how beautiful she is. I wish you had been this cute when you were that age. It would have made looking at you a little easier. Son, she is now your responsibility. You have to be a father, a hero, and a friend to her all at the same time.*

Maybe you are heart broken because she has Down syndrome. You probably sit up at night and cry about it. You are just like your mother. Suck it up. You bust your ass twice as hard to help her. You give her everything you possibly can give her, and then you work harder to give her more. You brought this beautiful girl into this world, and don't you think for a second you can give up on her. You stick it out and love her in a way you have never loved anyone else. This world can be cruel, so she needs you more than anyone else. This is your time to be a father, and just because she is not what you expected does not mean you can run out on her. She loves you, and it is time you love her like your Creator loves you. God gave you this little angel for a reason. so you give every part of your life to her."

You never have a chance to be a good father if you are not a present father. I believe the majority of problems with young men in this world is their lack of a strong father. My dad believed in responsibility, and that is not an easy code to live by. I had my own doubts and fears when my daughter was born, but you have to be committed for the future of your children. When you choose to leave a child behind, you are not escaping to an easier life, but instead, ruining a life you helped create. No child should have to grow up without a loving father in her life.

§

For a time after Marley's birth, I planned to walk away. It was a time when I could only see the negatives and darkness of having a child who was different. After a year of battling my own demons, my father helped me emerge from the murk of self loathing. He had been dead for several years, but on those nights I laid awake and contemplated my future, his voice clearly resonated in my mind:

> *"This is your baby girl, and she needs a father that will love her every single day of her life. She is not what you envisioned, but she will be a blessing to herself, you, and the world in more ways than you ever imagined! Be the best father you can be."*

- Jack Barr, Jr.

Dads of Disability

32

Predestined: The Journey of a Stay-at-Home Dad

The wildest, most imaginative script I could think of for my life never included a disabled child or being a stay-at-home dad. But then I discovered that the Lord had planned exactly that for me.

Our two boys were ages three and one when their twin siblings were born. Life was good and very normal for all of us. For me, normal meant that a certain amount of money had to be earned, and that my workplace accomplishments defined me. Especially now that I was a father of four, being the breadwinner made the most sense.

At work, I was the leader. I was in charge. Things happened because I was in command. I was the person everyone looked to provide guidance and specific answers. After all, manufacturing complex gears for the aerospace sector is no simple task. There are many moving pieces, complex factors, and unexpected events that you must react to on a daily basis despite your best proactive, preventative efforts. Little did I know that these skills would be just as critical in my next job.

Our first "diagnosis day" was 12 weeks after the twins were born. Savanna had epilepsy. Infantile Spasms was the primary diagnosis (other diagnosis days would follow). Within two days of entering the emergency room with our child, a pediatric neurologist said to Rebecca and me, "…you need to mourn the loss of your normal child. And, prepare your marriage, as 85 percent in your situation end in divorce." (There are controversies surrounding these numbers and their relation to different diagnoses, but Ken says that this is what the doctor told them. - *editor*)

We had a child with a severe brain malformation that resulted in the seizure disorders. The magnitude of her disability was largely unknown. There in the hospital room, the "normality" of our life disappeared forever.

The denial period was long for me as epilepsy can be such an invisible syndrome. However, Savanna's diagnosis was rife with peripheral and resultant complications, providing our family with many more "diagnosis days." With each new diagnosis, my denial lessened. This was for real, and it wasn't going away. And after several long, unanticipated hospital stays, we hit a brick wall with our family's work and lifestyle balance. My wife, Rebecca, and I both realized that one of us had to manage Savanna's care on a full-time basis.

My wife worked outside the home as well and remained steadfast that she would always work and would not just be a stay-at-home mom. Also, she has a history of allowing "the job" to take complete control of her time. This drove my desire to assume the role as primary caregiver to Savanna and the other children because I knew it was going to be overwhelming and full time.

The pivotal moment in my journey to becoming a stay-at-home dad came in a phone call from my boss two weeks into a hospital stay where Savanna nearly died from complications of aspiration pneumonia. While I was making it to work every day, I was often very late.

He called me one morning insincerely questioning my whereabouts. He couldn't understand why my wife could not just handle things without me. As I look back and reflect on this call, I realize it was not possible for this individual to understand that I was entrenched in an epic battle. Regardless, that call solidified the change of my relationship with the workplace and my acceptance of a new role.

While Savanna was in a stable honeymoon period of seizure control, we hastily ended our stay in California and moved to Texas. The decision matrix that led us to Houston was simple: appropriate care for Savanna and an economy that would allow us to thrive on one income. I was officially a stay-at-home dad (SAHD)!

Managing the daily tasks of three typically-developing children plus Savanna's needs did become overwhelming. Slowly, the Lord stripped away all things I once thought important. At first, I felt like I was losing my identity, but in reality, I was actually discovering it. After all the years I worked so diligently to build a career, just a few short months away from the workplace made those experiences seem far away and insignificant.

Then another diagnosis day: breakthrough complex partial seizures that would become dangerous and refractory to medical and nutritional therapies. In a matter of a few weeks, Savanna would transition from some electrographic activity to hundreds of clinical seizures per day, often requiring intervention beyond the scheduled medicines. I quickly became an expert in maintaining all aspects of Savanna's health. She was on the edge of a medically induced coma to protect her brain as the path to surgical treatment was planned.

Finally, in dramatic fashion, two rounds of surgical treatment over a five-month period provided seizure control. It was miraculous.

Now, nearly a year later, Savanna has blossomed into the little girl I never imagined she could be after her first diagnosis. I am honing my skill as a SAHD, which is much easier when not having a child seizing all day long. I am rededicating myself to this role, especially wanting to give more attention our other kids, whose needs often took a backseat to Savanna's over the past two years. And to add to the challenge, we now face another diagnosis for our Savanna: Autism Spectrum Disorder (ASD), unveiled by the control of the seizure disorder.

The Lord has blessed me with the ability to overcome obstacles in my own life to help Savanna and the rest of my family thrive. My blog, "Savanna's Journey," has helped me tremendously in processing my emotions, and in turn, has helped others realize they are not alone. Sanity, I find, is in the dark, secret place in my office where I can collect my thoughts.

I sometimes feel as if I have rescued my daughter. At other times, I feel I have done what any other father would do. I really enjoy being a SAHD but now feel our lifestyle balance needs adjustment if the family is to remain whole.

All of my workplace leadership experience has helped me take charge of our situation, open doors once closed for Savanna, and learn even more about what it means to be leader outside the workplace. I am eternally grateful to Rebecca for working outside the home and allowing me this experience.

Now, our entire family is at a new intersection. Savanna is thriving with therapies tailored to her specific needs. From the outside, nothing looks amiss. Seen from the inside, it is not so straightforward, and our marriage is clearly impacted. Friction between us grows as I continue to remain out of the workplace, and it sometimes feels that the "natural" or "expected" balance of family life is upside down. The journey to this point was tumultuous, but I must admit I really enjoy being a SAHD. If I must leave this post, the decision will come with some sadness.

I do not know what the future holds for me, or for us. But I do believe this path is not a random journey. It was predestined. In the script of our lives, we will arrive where we are supposed to be, intact, as a family.

- Kenneth Lininger

Dads of Disability

Transition

Dads die. Moms die. Children die. Siblings die. Friends and strangers die. And we all must prepare for death. Some prepare for it better than others.

How can we prepare for our death, for the possible death of a child, and for living a good life after a death?

Dads of Disability

33

Sara'sDad

Before we were married, my husband was the single dad of a daughter with developmental disabilities. He was angry with the responsibility, the reality, and the system. In addition to her disabilities, she had prolonged grief issues from losing her mother to breast cancer when she was only five, had few social skills, and resorted to stealing as a coping mechanism.

Dad was a boiler operator for a power plant, a job that he loved but that did not allow him to tuck his daughter in bed at night for two out of three weeks due to his swing-shift schedule. When he wasn't on day shift, she cried when she had to be left with one or the other of her grandmothers. He reluctantly gave up his promising career to find a 9-to-5 job that would provide the stability his daughter needed. The job he found paid significantly less than his power-plant job, was nothing he wanted to do, and made moving back to his childhood home the best option. His widowed mother was able to help with after school care, and there was a much-needed sense of family cohesiveness for all of them.

This situation was not ideal for my husband. It left him lonely, frustrated, and often emotionally empty. At this point in his life, he had not planned to share his daily life with his mother. She seemed to lean too heavily on him to fill the role of companion in his late father's absence. This was a family mired in grief and overwhelmed by the behaviors and needs of a child who was not identified with a specific diagnosis. The school district did the bare minimum in terms of special education and did not offer much in the way of supportive information. Determinations and decisions made at individualized education program (IEP) meetings were often outside the realm of his understanding, so he agreed to things that, in retrospect, he might not have agreed to had there been more resources to lean on.

His overuse of alcohol to cope with his situation had a negative effect on things at home. The school noted that his daughter's behavior had deteriorated and asked if there was something different going on in the family. Dad had an epiphany of sorts and realized that he needed to get himself together. He made a decision to focus on his daughter, promising himself that she would not fall by the wayside and get lost in the system if he could help it.

Together Dad and Daughter forged a stronger bond and began living again. They still carried a measure of grief, but Dad reached out for help, and they began a healing journey. There were still many ups and downs, but by his own admission, they luckily avoided the path of misery they were headed toward.

Dad began to warm up to his co-workers and made friends who made a job he really never wanted tolerable. He helped his daughter take baby steps toward a higher level of functioning and never stopped believing that given time and patience, she would continue to improve. Moving up to the middle school, he found staff who was interested in working with his daughter, and some good progress was made. They discovered camping in the great north woods of New Hampshire and went twice each summer, returning home in a better frame of mind for having escaped the everyday challenges to enjoy the slower pace of lakeside living, hiking, fishing, and breathtaking sunsets.

I had the good fortune to meet my husband at that job he never wanted. I sensed there was something extraordinary about him, and he intrigued me. My four-year-old scared him, and I had no personal experience with developmental disabilities. There were some on again, off again times, but eventually, we both knew that we had found a good place to be. He learned about my son's Irish-German-Italian-American temper tantrums, and I overcame my ignorance about disabilities.

This dad, who dedicated himself to saving his child, ended up saving himself. He had no way of knowing the twists and turns the road would take, but we came together as a family, marrying when Sara was 14. His daughter has a mom; my son has a dad. We have a well-blended, lovingly wacky, and boringly "normal" family.

I made friends who happened to be special education teachers. They told me what should be happening for our daughter, and we no longer accept the status quo. She is now 22 years old and has graduated from high school and a post-high school job training program. She has a part-time job as a housekeeper. We have all learned to look for the ability rather than to focus on the disability. She is flourishing because she has a dad who loves her and put her needs ahead of his own.

We are truly blessed to have this dad in our lives.

- Patricia Gray

(Patricia asked that the title of this piece be spelled "Sara'sDad" with no space. *-editor*)

34

A Son's Life Force

When I attended the monthly meetings of the *Seattle Area Fathers Network*, I was acutely aware that if another man were to accidentally walk into the room and see 20 or so of us sitting in a large circle, coffee cups in hand, he'd never be able to guess what we had in common. There was no external sign—just a bunch of guys—but we did share something. We all had a son or daughter with disabilities. And because of that circumstance, we better understood what each of us was dealing with. We all knew the frustrations and the fears and the rewards of trying to raise children who faced such daunting challenges. At these meetings, we didn't have to offer excuses or be falsely upbeat. We didn't have to pretend that things were going better than they were. We didn't have to put up a front of manly confidence. No, we could divulge our deepest fears, recount trying experiences, and nod in affirmation of what we dads were going through. It was a safe place.

I'd leave those meetings with the knowledge that I wasn't the only dad trying to deal with the most complex and demanding issues I'd ever faced. There were other men like me seeking to make the best of a demanding situation. The meetings were great. But when they ended, we each drove off to different parts of the Puget Sound, returning to our own lives. In my case, I was a single dad trying to raise Max, my six-year-old son, who had cerebral palsy.

His birth mom and I shared custody after we divorced when Max was about three and a half. He'd spend a week with me, a week with her until she decided, for reasons I couldn't fathom, to leave town, to leave her son. Max was five and a half at the time that she drove away. And I became a single dad of a son who used a wheelchair, couldn't speak, and required help for all of his basic living needs.

Like all the dads at our meetings, I'd never been instructed in the taking care of a child with special needs. If a psychic had addressed the me at age 30 and described what lay ahead, I would have laughed (or inwardly cried). Not only did I not know a thing about raising children, I certainly knew nothing about caring for someone who couldn't sit on his own, feed himself, or tell me he was cold.

From the moment Max was born (and quickly moved from the maternity room to the ICU), everything involving his care was harder and more demanding than what I saw other new dads experiencing. And the care became more complex with each passing month. I entered a world, more of a universe actually, almost beyond my comprehension. Max's condition was officially diagnosed at ten months: athetoid (involuntary movements) hypotonic (decreased muscle tone) cerebral palsy. Our new world included specialists and therapists and dieticians. Special equipment. Insurance dealings. And then came special education. And hospital admissions. But it also included Max and me finding ways for him to hold and throw a ball, not a baseball pitch in Little League, mind you, but a throw, nevertheless, that got a laugh out of him and a cheer out of me.

In my case, the new universe would also include divorce and single parenthood.

I was quite alone. Well, Max and I were alone. I didn't have any family in town. (I was living in Fort Collins, Colorado, at the time.) I didn't really ask for help from friends or workmates. Because Colorado State University had a program for physical therapists, I was able to hire students to babysit a couple of times a month, which gave me a needed break. And there was a monthly swimming program at a huge indoor pool, where a volunteer would take Max in the water and let him float around. (Max loved water.) Mostly, though, it was Max and me. Just Max and me.

In almost every way, what I had previously considered my "normal" life was limited by my son's condition. My work certainly suffered. My relationships with other adults were strained. I was tired, a lot. Transporting even a young and small Max still required much more than just popping him in his car seat. Once he had a wheelchair, it had to be disassembled and placed in the trunk (until I got a van, which still required special attention). What I would also discover over the years was an unexpected enlargement of positive experiences. I was introduced to a world most people only catch a glimpse of from the outside, a world of caring health care professionals who didn't believe in giving up, of other parents facing the same kind of challenges with dedication and heart, and, most importantly, of being the dad of an inspiring and loving son.

I had read that a parent of a child with disabilities goes through stages similar to that of a person facing death: confusion, disbelief, and eventually acceptance. Sort of. I moved through those stages but also discovered that an incident or even a word from someone could trigger a return of the earlier stages. Even someone asking, "How do you manage?" could set me back.

My life wasn't supposed to have gone this way. A writer, a performer, a person without deep responsibilities… now responsible for the life of a physically-challenged little boy. Where was my script? Where was the Hollywood happy ending?

Along the way, I learned more about myself and what I was capable of achieving. I now had duties, including becoming an advocate and aide for someone who could not speak for himself. For example, I learned how to push Max's wheelchair in a shopping mall or down a street knowing everyone was looking—but not looking—at us and be able to keep on walking. It was hard to make eye contact with people who looked away as they walked towards us. I'm not sure when the change occurred, but after several years, it began to feel more natural to be wheeling Max around. I learned how not to feel ashamed that I was the father of a son who wasn't like all the other children we passed.

Didn't Max deserve the right to be out and about? In some ways, I began to see us as examples of a new way of letting people with disabilities be a part of the fabric of society. Max would not spend his time inside his room. He and I would go out and explore the world to the best of our abilities. In an hour we could drive from Fort Collins to Rocky Mountain National Park, which had some wheelchair accessible paths. We even made it around Bear Lake, which has a path, of sorts, but required more push and pull on my part to navigate.

There were some terrific women who were willing to share time with me (and that meant with Max as well). They were able to see beyond Max's physical limitations, to accept him for who he was. He, in turn, offered his winning smile.

My son, physically challenged as he was, had a great laugh and eyes that could give you a look of such deepness that you could see he was an old soul. And despite his many challenges, he genuinely seemed to be thrilled to be alive. It took a while, but over time I began to see Max as a kind of teacher. If anyone deserved to be depressed and glum, he would certainly be a candidate. But he wasn't. His attitude began to rub off on me. True, I was tired from work and caregiving. And I went in and out of feeling sorry for myself. But Max would bring me back to a central essence of what it is to be alive. And to be loved. And to be in the here and now. Max might have been limited in body but not in spirit.

A half year after his birth mom left, I had a conversation with Max. I asked him if he wanted to move and where he'd like to go. As much as I loved Fort Collins and Colorado, the winters were long. "How about Seattle?" I asked. Max didn't say no. (Actually, with his limited communication skills, this was a one-sided conversation. But, Max was adaptable, and we would be in this change together.)

I found a job opportunity, so we relocated. Again, we were a team. And I thought that would be our fate. Father and son. I'd drive up and down Aurora Avenue, Max behind me in the van's second row of seats. I'd sigh. On clear days, Mt. Rainier would shine in the distance, beckoning.

When I was least expecting it, when I was adapting to Team Max and Me, a woman I had thoughts about dating demurred in that role. But she played matchmaker and said there was a special someone I should meet. Max was coming out of some serious hospitalizations and still recovering. I hesitated. For several months. One night, I came across the woman's phone number and called. Maybe it was time to re-explore Life.

Lane agreed to meet for dinner at an ale house. I got lost finding the place and showed up late, but she was still there. We were drawn to each other. And she didn't pull away when I introduced her to Max. Ten months later, Lane and I married. Max wore a coat and tie to the outdoor wedding overlooking Puget Sound.

Lane became Max's mom. Then we added a baby sister, Lila, to the family. Max lived another 14 years, years filled with extreme health issues yet also a lot of fun times, including camping, travel, and daily routines, all buoyed by his bountiful life force.

Max was born a mystery, and he died a mystery. In between, he faced more challenges than any other person I have ever known. And yet, after every hospitalization, every dance with near death, he would be back at his home, attentive, playful, alive.

I wonder now what kind of man I would be if Max had not been my son. Better rested perhaps, but less aware of the power of love. This I now know: I am a richer person, more caring, more thoughtful, more appreciative, for having had Max in my life.

- *Martin Perlman*

Dads of Disability

35

Mickey Won't Die, But We Will

My son Tim, who at 46 is still a slightly magical person, believes that you can make the world as you wish it to be. He says that when he turns 65, he and Grammie will retire and live at the beach. (Grammie is 95 now. At that point, she would be 114 years old.)

Aging is something that happens so slowly that we don't notice differences from day to day. We may notice the changes in others but are sometimes surprised to actually see it in ourselves. For example, I don't feel much different than I did twenty years ago, but when did my hair go gray? This seemed to disturb Tim recently as he told me I should have brown hair, not gray.

How can we help Tim prepare for the inevitable changes that will come for those he loves the most? We have worked hard to build a circle of support for him, so that his life will always be the same quality that he now enjoys. This year on our family vacation, we will travel to Disney World to spend a few days with the truly ageless Mickey Mouse. Can we figure out how to stop the passage of time as Mickey has?

We have tried to limit Tim's exposure to death to just a few people who were important in his life. He has been curious and thoughtful in those situations. When his grandfather passed away, we took him to the funeral home before the opening of calling hours. We were the only people in the building. He carefully went up to the casket, and touched the body. I guess it was his way of assuring himself that the person was no longer here. He suddenly said, "Glasses, glasses!" We located his grandfather's glasses and put them on. Now grandfather was ready for whatever journey he was about to take.

Tim's last act with his grandfather was to take a photo. With his photographic memory and the pictures that he constantly takes to document his favorite actions, Tim is able to preserve and replay important moments and happy times in the past. When the inevitable time comes, will these images help him deal effectively with the death of his closest loved ones?

We believe that those who have passed on still have a place in the world. So each summer, we take a trip to the family plot where his grandfather is buried. It is in a tiny cemetery in a small town. When we arrive, Tim goes to check the marker that indicates his grave. He brushes off the stone, and removes the pine needles that may have fallen into the letters carved in the granite. On his first trip there, after cleaning his grandfather's stone, he noticed another marker right beside it. It has his grandmother's name, with the date to be carved upon her passing. He lamented, "Oh, Grammie!" We hastily pointed out that Grammie was with us and still very much alive. He was quite relieved.

And how will Tim deal with his own aging? So far, the physical changes that accompany age have been subtle (for example, he has developed a widow's peak), but that, too, will change. It is hard to think of him as a senior citizen, with the accompanying aches and pains.

As for the future, Tim has adapted to a variety of different living situations up to this point, so we remain optimistic for him. Our hope is that he will look at the images of times past in his mind's eye and in his myriad photo albums and take comfort in remembering us as we were.

- Dave Hackett

Dads of Disability

36

Smartphone Tears

For many years, I have attended an annual, statewide support conference for families with members who have disabilities. This is a place where families and individuals with disabilities come together for a weekend of informative sessions, commiseration, swimming, and for some, letting go and drinking. It's a pretty big affair and something that many of us look forward to all year.

We feel a sense of comfort seeing and celebrating the same faces year after year and mourning the absence, and sometimes unfortunately the loss, of others. There are folks who have had and are having an impact at the local, state, and even national level for our families. Also attending are dads, moms, grandparents, caregivers and service providers, and young and adult children who just do their day-to-day best to learn how to survive and thrive.

Last spring was the 13th year I attended this conference. And I did two things I rarely do during the rest of the year: (1) Have more than one drink (I am usually a half-a-beer kind of guy) and (2) Sing karaoke (I am usually an only-sing-at-home kind of guy). It feels safe letting down one's guard in front of a large group of people with such an intimate affinity to families with experiences like ours.

After hearing a large number of wonderful interpretations of some popular songs and participating in a few myself, it was getting close to closing time. Imagine that! Me closing down a bar. That doesn't really happen a lot anymore. (Okay. It never happens anymore.) By that time, I was sitting down in a sheen of karaoke sweat at the back of the bar and getting ready to leave. The Karaoke DJ called last song, and a bunch of the rowdiest and best-known of our annual compatriots got up to lock arms and sing a song. I'd have to ask someone what the song was, because I don't remember. And the song they sang isn't really the point anyway.

Before I continue, let me describe a father in this group I have known only casually over the past decade. Actually, I have only known him in the context of this conference and preparations for it. He is a heavy-set fellow, quick to laugh and hug and smile and cry. This is a guy known in this group as someone who is willing to do almost anything! More than once he got all his hair cut off to support fund raising for this conference. He is a hard-working, blue-collar guy, smart, funny, and a man whom everyone likes. I respect him a whole lot, although we are really different kinds of men. He really isn't the kind of guy you walk up and say, "I really respect you a lot."

I have seen him do many amazing things. The one I marvel at is that even after his disabled daughter passed away, he continued to volunteer for and be a part of this conference in a deeply meaningful way. He is an amazing man. After losing his daughter, I am not sure how he kept on in life at all, much less with this conference. Strength is packaged in an amazing number of ways.

So, back to closing time at karaoke. The last song was playing, and everyone singing it at the front of the bar (there were probably dozens by the end) was swaying back and forth to the rhythm. And this man, organizer, father, karaoke-ist, took out his smartphone, set it to a picture of his daughter, and held it above his head while swaying. It was extremely touching, and I am sure that anyone who knew his story shed a tear or two.

The simple act of this regular man, continuing on in a way that I am not sure I could, standing there with our peers singing, swaying, celebrating, and memorializing his daughter. And I lost it.

Not "a few tears and smiles" kind of lost it. Not a "quiet, internal sobbing" lost it. Not an "odd chirping cry" kind of lost it. It was a "loud, heart-wrenching, snot-forming, visceral bawl that hit me so hard I had to step out of the bar" kind of lost it.

This was "an over a dozen years of doctor visits, school meetings, emergency room visits, family explanations, supportive community member, genetic diagnosis, watching child ask to come home from the psychiatric hospital, no more than three hours of uninterrupted sleep per night, separation and divorce, residential school placement, insulting politicians, broken bone, advocating for legislation, going broke, not knowing how to live" kind of cry that was just not going to stop anytime soon.

How could this man go on like this? His late daughter, present only in an angelic, ghostly light seen by all on his smartphone? What if that happens to my child?

And then my feeling of guilt for sobbing for the false equivalency of my son entering a residential school placement less than a year before with a child pre-deceasing her father. Then full circle to every possible fear, anxiety, guilt, and happiness that I had not permitted myself to process fully for almost 14 years. I really had never mourned in steeping-hot, fast-flowing, and profoundly deep tears this way ever, before or since. And perhaps never again.

After the song ended and people started to come out of the bar, I kind of hid a bit behind some vendor booths on a couch. I was still distraught. Two guys I know pretty well saw what was going on. And despite what was becoming embarrassing (I mean, people were leaving the bar to go back to their rooms and walking past me), I continued to bawl. Then a guy I had just met (although I knew his activist wife) came over. And then a fourth guy, friends with one of the first ones (but who didn't have a child with a disability) came over.

Although we were in public, the moment quickly became private as folks from the bar walked by on their way to their rooms. But I sat on the couch, cried, and shared private thoughts with these guys in relative safety and with the support that only another dad of disability could provide. We talked for 30 minutes about some really intense and private stuff. I calmed down and cleaned up. Then we went back to a room for an after-party where I sobered up. And there I reveled in the amazing power of fathers helping fathers. And of mothers who saw what was going on, letting their husbands help, and offering non-judgmental hugs to me as well.

The funny thing is, I am pretty sure that the father who raised his smartphone in memory of his daughter has no idea the impact his power as a father and a man has on me.

- Gary Dietz

Dads of Disability

37

My Brother Ernie

Now age 70, I am a financial and insurance advisor for a major firm, an active Rotarian, and a Vietnam veteran. My older brother, Ernest (Ernie), passed away five years ago at age 72. Ernie had lifelong intellectual, emotional, and physical challenges and lived at home until age 18.

Through high school, Ernie was tutored on a regular basis by a Catholic diocese brother. (Remember, this was before special education laws in the U.S.) When our parents could no longer manage at home, Ernie moved to a full-time care facility. He was a resident of the Concord State Hospital and then moved to Greenbriar, a long-term care facility, both in New Hampshire.

My parents visited Ernie as regular as clockwork until they passed away. When I contemplate our father's relationship with Ernie, I remembered that I was very young when Ernie moved into an institutional setting. What I realized was that Father showed the family that you don't leave family members behind. That whatever happens, you take care of them. That love and respect do not stop because a person has mental or physical challenges.

After our parents passed away, I became Ernie's guardian. Our brother, and later our nephew, were both New Hampshire-based medical doctors and provided Ernie with primary care. Trips home on holidays continued late into Ernie's life and visits by me and other family members with him at Greenbriar continued on a regular basis throughout his life.

§

About three weeks before Ernie passed away, I stopped by Greenbriar and went to his room. He wasn't there. When I went to the nurse's station and asked if they knew where Ernie was, they said he was on the porch. I took a walk to the porch (it was enclosed and safe). He wasn't there. So I went back to the nurse's station and asked if they had any other ideas about where Ernie was.

"Sometimes he goes down to physical therapy," one nurse said. So I left the nurse's station, went down to PT, and looked around. Ernie wasn't there.

"He was here about a half hour ago, but then he left," they told me. I asked if they had any idea where he was.

"Sometimes he hangs out over at the administration offices." Ernie used to go there often and just sit outside. So I went over to the administration offices. I asked someone if he was there, and they said he was there about 15 minutes ago. "But we have no idea where he is now."

I looked around some more but couldn't find him. He was in the building somewhere, but I just kept missing him.

So I left. I knew he would be okay. It was a safe place.

When I went back a week later for a visit, I asked Ernie where he was the week before. I told him I had stopped by but couldn't find him. He said that he had gone to visit every floor. I guess I must have just missed him by a just a few minutes at every location.

The week before he passed away, I visited and again, my final visit. He was not in his room. So I walked over to see if he was in physical therapy. When I looked down the hall, I could see the back of his wheelchair going into PT. This was Sunday, so there was only one person there.

I walked up and watched Ernie slowly going across the floor in his wheelchair. He got to the other wall, turned around, and then he saw me, "Hi Conrad!"

He started to come back toward me, and I walked and met him half way. As I greeted him, it was the first time I saw Ernie with stuff on his face; it was kind of dirty. So I cleaned him up. After I was done helping him, he said, "Please bring me back to my room."

So I brought him back to his room. It was at two o'clock in the afternoon. He asked me to help him into bed. I said "Ernie, it's only two o'clock. You don't want to go to bed now."

Ernie responded "I'm old, and I'm tired. When you are old and you are tired, you go to bed." Those were my brother Ernie's last words to me.

Later, after he was gone, it hit me that he had been going around Greenbriar looking at the whole facility. Seeing everyone he knew. In his final weeks, he had gone to see everybody and everything at Greenbriar. I believe, in his own way, he was saying goodbye, perhaps without realizing it. Or maybe he did.

- Conrad Dionne

Dads of Disability

Coda

Humans are pretty good at adapting. But sometimes we need a kick in the pants.

There are often contexts where we need to adapt the language we use around and about our young and adult children.

We find ourselves needing to adapt our dreams for us and our families when we are presented with challenges.

Perhaps we need to learn to adapt in the way a young child does when first exposed to disability—by being curious and honest and unafraid and unconditionally accepting.

Dads of Disability

38

Adapted Views

He asks what I am doing
when I stare at the sea. I tell him
I am thinking about how far my eye
can travel, the seamless layers
in a Rothko painting, the sacred spaces
only lost sailors claim.

I watch his green eyes gray,
know the need to simplify—
adjust for the loss
behind his childlike smile;
so I tell him I love the colors,
the pinks and purples
in a sunset sky, the waves that splash
white against the rocks.

He says he likes it best when I do that.

- Patricia Wallace Jones

Dads of Disability

39

Roles They are A-Changin'

A father of a child with a disability is not the same father he would be if he had no children with disabilities. How can we help others who will come after us be better prepared than we were? How can we help society be better prepared for who we are and better support us?

What if we, as fathers of all ages, with children of all ages, with disabilities of all types, would decide to pro-actively break through annoying and hurtful stereotypes about us as men and our children as people? (I don't know about you, but the next time I am called a "special ed parent" by a principal, as if my role as parent is defined solely by that, I will revolt.)

But there are other stereotypes to deal with first. You know, the ones that constantly appear in media in ways you can probably recite in your sleep. The "inspirational memes" that, while true, often merely serve to replace more serious dialog about needed change. (It *is* really cool that the disabled towel boy was called into the game and threw a 3-pointer. But perhaps we should be equally focused on that boy the other 364 days of the year?)

The memes continue. The "unfortunate" family. The "adorable" handicapped child. (Are there ever *unattractive* disabled children in stock photos?) Can you imagine a fundraiser in the media for a family whose patriarch was unappealing and didn't radiate enthusiasm? Don't fundraisers for children of grumpy parents deserve press?

I don't know about you, but I am tired of these stereotypical messages and images in the paper and on TV. It *is* nice to make people feel good, but to have no other goal short of making other people feel good—or less guilty—misses an essential point. These memes can make us all miss an opportunity to affect change.

Disability is a part of life. We would all be better served to understand that deeply. I was at a seminar once, and the leader asked, "Raise your hand if you have a disabled child. Now raise your hand if you have a disabled parent. Now raise your hand if someone in your extended family has a disability. Now raise your hand if you have a close friend that is disabled. Now, raise your hand if you think you could be disabled in some way before you die." The point was clear. Eventually, we all will deal with some form of disability someday, in some way.

Fathers' roles are changing. Why is it still a big deal that a father chooses to stay at home to raise a disabled child while the mother works outside of the home? Why do fathers bringing their children to the hospital for appointments often still get treated as the "second tier" parent? Roles are changing faster than laws, the courts, the medical system, and our employers are. Faster than some segments of society can react to. Could we dads of disability and our families help affect change that will benefit not just us, but every family, disability or not?

Dads of disability should have authentic messages, and help the media and our communities focus on images of unity and reality, not fluff and things that make people think, "They are them, and we are us. Thank goodness I am not them!" Not everyone has the skills to engage media, or the time or wherewithal to speak at a statehouse. But all of us have a responsibility to speak up when a child is illegally restrained or controlled in a school setting. To write a letter to the editor to call "BS" when we see it. To stand up for others' children when necessary and not turn a blind eye. When we mobilize our strength publicly as men and as dads of disability, it becomes easier to replace the sanitized, happy-assed, inspiration-porn that often masquerades as advocacy for families like ours after editing by an uninspired or uneducated media producer.

I dream that whether at the statehouse, the doctor's office, at home, or at work, we can break through the expected and trite media memes and encourage the general population to think differently about our families and, in my particular dream, a father's role in our kinds of families. I dream of getting people to understand that disability can happen in *any* family of *any* political or *any* economic stripe. I dream that we dads of disability will help create and participate in systems in our society where fathers can "do it all" at work and at home in support of our children and spouses (just like moms!). I dream that changes will benefit all kinds of families, whether they have family members with disabilities or not.

As women's and mothers' roles justifiably change, there must be a parallel adjustment in expectation and acceptance of father's and male caregivers' changing roles. Roles can't change in a vacuum. We men must be there to support women as their roles evolve. And women must be a part of helping men redefine caregiving and parenting.

In this volume alone, we saw evidence of change in expectations and actions regarding fathers that we likely wouldn't have seen so much or at all in the near past. Reading the essays with this filter in mind, we can see evidence of these changed attitudes.

- Damian demanded to be talked to and heard by nurses and doctors as an equal parent to the mother, not to be ignored until his wife recovered from surgery.

- Nate came to understand he needed to listen more carefully to his second wife about his new child and what the role of a male advocate required.

- Hal realized he must re-evaluate his fatherly approach and definition of manhood for him and his son, regardless of his long-held assumptions and those of his extended family.

- Elizabeth constructed a home life with her ex-husband to put the children first, and he was willing to put the children first as well in this unusual living arrangement.

- Ken and his wife had to re-evaluate the implications of having a stay-at-home dad in their family and acknowledge that the financial power of a couple can be fluid.

- Jack thought about running away, but didn't. And as much as the media or some support groups may point out that "men leave" disabled children—more often than not, they don't.

- Martin stepped up as a single dad.

- Mike and his spouse made the conscious decision to adopt children with disabilities.

I dream that the changing roles of mothers and fathers will allow them *both* to powerfully and publicly participate in not just the physical support (food, shelter, clothing) of children with disabilities, but also in their emotional lives and daily care. I dream that dads and moms of all stripes can add equally to the dialog and exposure of disability in family life in all forms of media in broader, more inclusive, and more realistic ways. I dream that this will help us all move toward the next phase of addressing disability in our society. Its acceptance as everyday. As typical. As a natural part of life.

- Gary Dietz

Dads of Disability

40

Lila the Philosopher

Lila was almost 4 years old when this story happened.

Lila: Do all people have all their parts?

Lila's Dad: Well, most people do, but some don't. (A discussion about birth defects, amputation, etc. ensued.) So some people don't have all of their parts.

Lila: But they're still people, right Daddy?

Lila's Dad: Oh yes, Lila.

Lila: They're still people. That's the most important part.

- Lila

Dads of Disability

41

About the Authors

The biographies of essayists and poets are listed in the order of their appearance in this volume.

MaryAnn Campion is the founding director of the Master of Science Program in Genetic Counseling at Boston University School of Medicine. Originally from Gainesville, GA, she received a bachelor's degree in psychology from Furman University and a master's degree in genetic counseling from the University of South Carolina. She is currently pursuing a doctorate in educational leadership and policy from Boston University and is a practicing prenatal genetic counselor at Boston Medical Center. She lives in Boston, MA with her husband and two sons.

Gary Dietz is a father, a writer, an entrepreneur, and a marketing guy. He lives in New Hampshire.

Beth Gallob is a storyteller, entrepreneur, and caregiver for her husband of 40 years. She loves words, dogs, sister-friends, and champagne (there's always something to celebrate!). Her goals in life are to practice loving kindness and to laugh every day. Her hero is her late father, a WWII vet who embraced a brand new life at 91.

Marly Youmans is the author of eleven books of poetry and fiction. Recent books are: a post-apocalyptic adventure in blank verse, *Thaliad*, with Phoenicia Publishing; collections of poems, *The Foliate Head* from Stanza Press and *The Throne of Psyche* from Mercer; and a novel, *A Death at the White Camellia Orphanage*, (The Ferrol Sams Award; Silver Award, ForeWord BOTYAs). Books in 2014 are *Glimmerglass* and a reprint of *Catherwood*. *Maze of Blood* will appear in 2015. A South Carolina native, Marly has lived in Cooperstown, NY with her husband and three children for the past 14 years. Marly blogs at http://thepalaceat2.blogspot.com/

Damian Boyd is a passionate communicator, visionary leader, and pastor. Damian published his first book, *College Impact*, in 2010. He leads Vertical Church in the urban, college community of Historic West End/Vine City of Atlanta, GA. Damian and his wife, Zarat, celebrate over 14 years of marriage and over 9 years of raising their son, Damian Jr., who is a gifted, musical child with complex medical needs. He loves his family deeply.

Nate Weiner is a semi-retired custom motorcycle painter-house builder who has lived in New Hampshire for over 30 years. His passion for riding motorcycles on the race track is only surpassed by his love for his wife and son. These days he spends his time building a new energy efficient home to secure his son's living arrangements in the future.

Robbi Nester lives and writes in Southern California. She is the author of a chapbook, *Balance* (White Violet Press, 2012) and the editor of an anthology of NPR and PBS poems, *The Liberal Media Made Me Do It!*, forthcoming on Nine Toes Press, a subdivision of Lummox Press. Her collection of poetry, *A Likely Story*, will be published in summer 2014 by Moon Tide Press. Robbi has written on the subjects in this book before. Her essays have appeared in *Easy to Love, But Hard To Raise* (2011), an anthology and blog about raising children with disabilities.

Mike Kenny is a humor columnist for The Glendale Star and Peoria Times newspapers near Phoenix, AZ. His latest book, *The Man in the Garlic Tuxedo*, is available for you to buy. Yes, you! While you're there (the Internet), feel free to buy his first book, *So, Do You Like ... Stuff?*, or check out his blog of the same name for free. Then, follow him on Twitter, @mikekennystuff. Then, take a nap. You've had a long, productive day.

Chas Waitt spends most of his time outdoors with his wife and son and their two dogs. One of their favorite pastimes is ice fishing in the Alberta, Canada, winters. He strives for self improvement and is a motivated father for his son.

Ron Budway, Sr. resides in southern New Hampshire in a semi-retired and somewhat somnambulant state after a career as a Chief Financial Officer. He occupies his days doing adjunct teaching at the local community college, playing golf badly, and playing Texas Hold'em poker every chance he gets. He lives with Charlotte, his lovely wife of 45 years, and their fourth youngest child, Matthew.

Doug Keating lives in the Boston suburbs with his wife Crystal, his 8-year-old daughter, Sylvia, and his 5-year-old son, Charlie. This is his first published essay.

Elizabeth J. (Ibby) Grace is an Autistic scholar and activist and holds a position as Assistant Professor of Education at National Louis University in Chicago, where she lives in the suburbs with her lovely wife and two magnificent two-year-old sons. She blogs at http://tinygracenotes.blogspot.com and is an editor on *i.e.: inquiry in education* (digitalcommons.nl.edu/ie/) and http://NeuroQueer.blogspot.com Her writing can also be found in the books *Loud Hands* and *Both Sides of the Table: Autoethnographies of Educators Learning and Teaching With/In [Dis]ability.* A founding member of Autistic Activism Collective, Ibby is also on the Board of Directors of Autism Women's Network, working on *DIVERgent: when disability and feminism collide.*

Karl Williams has published two books with leaders in the self-advocacy movement (the civil rights work of people with intellectual disabilities); his play, based on one of these, *Lost In A Desert World: The Autobiography Of Roland Johnson*, premiered in San Diego. Songs from Williams' six CDs have aired on NBC, FOX, cable, and German TV, as well as on SIRIUS and earth-bound radio stations around the world. http://www.karlwilliams.com

Sam Smith is editor of *The Journal* (once *of Contemporary Anglo-Scandinavian Poetry*), publisher of *Original Plus* books. He was born in Blackpool in 1946 and is now living in Maryport, Cumbria, UK. A freelance writer now, he has been a psychiatric nurse, residential social worker, milkman, plumber, laboratory analyst, groundsman, sailor, computer operator, scaffolder, gardener, painter and decorator... working at anything, in fact, which has paid his rent, enabled him to raise his three daughters, and which hasn't got too much in the way of his writing. He now has several poetry collections and novels to his name. His web site is http://thesamsmith.webs.com/

Tom Lawrence, Jr. is a proud father and storyteller. He lives with his family in the North Georgia mountains, often wears a kilt, and throws heavy things for fun.

Patricia Wallace Jones is a life-long artist who began writing poetry after retiring and moving from the Midwest to the northern California coast. After becoming the mother of a son who had severe intractable seizures and cognitive and behavioral disabilities following a bout with H-flu meningitis, she changed careers and worked until retirement as a disability rights advocate for persons with disabilities and their families with Missouri's Protection and Advocacy System and later as Co-Director of MPACT, Missouri's statewide federally funded parent training center. Her art is in local shows and private collections, and her poems and/or art have appeared in *The Avatar Review, Lily, Tilt, Lucid Rhythms, The Guardian, 14 by 14, The Chimaera, The Flea, Wordgathering, The Shit Creek Review, The Centrifugal Eye* and *Victorian Violet Press.*

Hal Hanlin has tried everything from real estate agent, to stock broker, to serving as a Sergeant in the United States Marine Corps. He has found his calling as a video game producer. He lives in the outskirts of Austin, TX with his wife, son, daughter, father, and two cats. They have learned many lessons about patience in this living arrangement, along with a healthy respect for honesty, forgiveness, and "me-time."

John C. Mannone, nominated three times for the Pushcart, has work in *Raven Chronicles, Synaesthesia, 3elements Review, The Baltimore Review, Prime Mincer, Pirene's Fountain, The Pedestal, Tipton Poetry Journal, Wordgathering: Journal of Disability Poetry, Bloomsbury Publishing, Bethany House Publishers,* and others. He's the poetry editor for *Silver Blade* and *Abyss & Apex,* and an adjunct professor of physics in east Tennessee. Visit *The Art of Poetry* at http://jcmannone.wordpress.com

Viki Gayhardt has a degree in Human Services and has worked for nearly two decades as an autism family support specialist. She serves on the New Hampshire Council for Autism Spectrum Disorders as the Governor's designee, and recently started a family-run auto repair business with her husband. Gayhardt is also a singer-songwriter and has collaborated with Musicians for a Cause in the Songs4Autism Campaign. She released her first full length CD *Unguarded Heart* in 2011. You can learn more about her at www.vikigayhardt.com

Elizabeth O'Neill is a writer and mother of two girls. Her work has been published in the *Red River Review, Moxie* magazine, and *That Takes Ovaries! Bold Females and Their Brazen Acts*. She lives in Kansas City and is an active member of the Autism Society of America and the National Alliance on Mental Illness (NAMI), the nation's largest grassroots mental health organization.

Pam Hauck worked as a drug and alcohol counselor for sixteen years until she flew backwards off a treadmill and sustained a spinal injury at S1 and S2. Now, she writes from home. Her work has been published in *The Women of the Web: Anthology of Poems, The Tactile Mind Quarterly of the Signing Community, The Phoenix: The World's Oldest Recovery Newspaper,* and various other print and online venues. Feel free to contact her at pam.hauck@gmail.com

Carrie Cariello is the author of *What Color Is Monday, How Autism Changed One Family for the Better*. She lives in Southern New Hampshire with her husband, Joe, and their five children. Carrie is a regular contributor to *Autism Spectrum News* has been featured on *WordPress, The Huffington Post*, and *Parents.com*. She has a Masters in Public Administration from Rockefeller College and an MBA from Canisius College in New York. You can learn more about Carrie and her journey with marriage, autism, and motherhood at http://www.carriecariello.com By her best estimate, she and Joe have changed roughly 16,425 diapers.

Bobbie Guice has been married to Cliff for 35 years. They are proud parents of two daughters as well as son

Kevin, who was featured in this essay. They are also grandparents of four granddaughters. Bobbie has been the primary caregiver for Kevin, diagnosed with Cerebral Palsy and numerous other diagnoses, for 26 years. She works part time for a non-profit legal aid clinic in Orange County, CA.

Natalia Nodiff is a passionate student leader, writer, artist, activist, club president, and mentor. She is currently working on her Bachelor's Degree in Behavioral Science and is a member of Phi Theta Kappa Honor Society at Bunker Hill Community College. Her long-term goal is to work in public health to affect major changes within the mental healthcare system. She is an experienced practitioner of meditation, and a strong advocate of mindfulness and its role in well-being. She lives in Boston, MA with her pet guinea pig, Coco. This is Natalia's first publication, and she gives special thanks to Bob Higgins for inspiring her contribution.

Jeff Howe is the director of the media innovation program at Northeastern University and a visiting scholar at MIT Media Lab. His work has appeared in *The New Yorker, The New York Times, Wired* magazine, and many other publications. His last book was *Crowdsourcing: How the Power of the Crowd is Driving the Future of Business*, based on a Wired article that coined the term crowdsourcing.

Paul Rivard resides in New Hampshire with his wife and three children. He is currently a field service manager for a company located in the Boston Area. His daily life is always full of surprises—he and his family own two dogs, two cats, a leopard gecko, and a fish. He wouldn't change a thing. You can read more about his daughter Megan's disability at www.dup15q.org

Raymond Kent is an educator, lecturer, presenter, author, artist, and technology consultant specializing in the built environment with efforts to provide a more sustainable way of life. His international exploits have received many accolades but it is his son, Parker, who keeps him grounded. You can find him on Twitter @sustaintechllc, #sustaintechllc on his Facebook Page 'Sustainable Technologies Group, LLC' or on LinkedIn at http://www.linkedin.com/in/raykent/

Paul Digby Paul Digby is a composer and artist originally from the UK, but now living in Ohio, USA. He has been married for 12 years to his lovely American artist wife, Lynn. He has two children from his first marriage in 1979 and two stepchildren from his second marriage. Paul is retired now but worked in design and computer systems until life became too busy for him to do that any more.

Matthew Salesses is the author, most recently, of *I'm Not Saying, I'm Just Saying*. He has written for *The New York Times Motherlode* blog, *NPR Code Switch, Salon, The Rumpus, Hyphen Magazine*, and elsewhere. He is the fiction editor and a contributing writer at *The Good Men Project*. Follow him on Twitter @salesses or find him at http://www.matthewsalesses.com.

Rusty Earl is a documentary film maker based in northeast Kansas. His work can be seen at https://vimeo.com/rustyearl He is the proud father of two boys with special needs, Hyrum (Autism) and Nathaniel (9p-8q+ Chromosome Disorder) He is also the father of two girls with their own special needs.

Jack L. Barr Jr. is a teacher at the International Community School in Bangkok, Thailand. Jack and his wife Jana established the *If They Had A Voice* campaign, which has been covered by CNN, The Miracle Channel, and Giuliana Rancic. Their daughter Marley, who has Down syndrome, has altered their beliefs about disabilities and motivated them to share their story with other families. Jack will be publishing his first book in the summer of 2014.

Kenneth Lininger was born and raised in Louisville, KY and now calls Houston, TX his home. He is a stay-at-home dad to four wonderful kids and is the husband of an awesome lady. You can find him blogging at http://www.savannalininger.wordpress.com and http://www.somesahdexperiences.wordpress.com.

Patti Gray is a New Hampshire native, a breast cancer survivor, and has been married to Joe for seven years. She is a mom to a blended family of four children from ages 12 to 26. She has been a medical laboratory technologist for 33 years and is also a Mary Kay consultant. In her spare time she is the supervisor of Sara's self-directed services program. Patti also sits on New Hampshire's Region 3 Family Support Council. She loves creative writing, camping, boating and "forced family fun" days.

Martin Perlman was parent, advocate and caregiver for his son, Max (1990-2013). He has been writing since the sixth grade when his teacher assigned the class the challenge of creating stories using the weekly spelling lists. Martin has gone on to write short stories, humor pieces, essays, features, and news stories. He is currently working on a batch of children's stories and a whimsical novel about blogging written in blog form. A future project awaits: *The Max Story.* His blog site, *Thinking Out Loud,* is at http://marperl.blogspot.com Martin lives in Seattle with his wife, Lane, and his daughter, Lila. (Not the same Lila in the chapter *Lila the Philosopher. - editor*)

Dave Hackett has been a dad since the 1960's, when autism was rare (1 in 2500 births). With his wife, Louise, Dave defined *Advocacy in New Hampshire* and founded the *New Hampshire Autism Society.* In addition to their son, they have a daughter who has been very active in promoting disability rights. Currently, Dave works as a legislative consultant on disability issues.

Conrad Dionne is the sixth of seven children. He has been married for 49 years and has three children and four grandchildren. He is a New Hampshire native who has worked in the financial services industry for fifty years. He is an active member of the Rotary Club and a proud Vietnam War veteran who served in the Army from 1964 to 1970 and was awarded a Bronze Star medal.

Lila is a little girl who lives in Massachusetts with her sister, her father, and her mother. She says intelligent things.

Dads of Disability

42

Acknowledgments

Thanks to my son Alexander, who is the light of my life. This project is in large part due to a silent promise I made to him after he enrolled in a specialized residential school and moved there during the weekdays, thus changing our lives and family dynamic dramatically. I promised him I would take care of myself so I will be around and healthy to care for him and us long as I can. And this book, as hard as it has been practically and financially, was a large part of my path back to myself after the events leading up to his transition. Alexander, I love you very much.

Thanks to MaryAnn Campion of Boston University, one of the first people to return my phone calls when I was researching the need for this project. If she hadn't answered that call, this book might not exist. She offered her support, she followed through many times in e-mail and on the phone, and she wrote an amazing foreword.

Thanks to Casey Silvestri, who worked remotely with me in time and space during her final month of high school (she graduated the same high school as I did, *exactly* 30 years later) to create the marketing animation for this project. I am honored to have worked with her well before she receives her first Academy Award, which she undoubtedly will. (I hope she remembers me in her acceptance speech.) Watch the animation at http://blog.dadsofdisability.com/animation

Thanks to those who believed in this project enough to pledge to an initial Kickstarter project (that was not funded successfully) and then to a follow-up Indiegogo project (that was successful). The money helped, but more than crowd*funding*, I was able to crowd*source* many of the essayists that appear. The power of the crowd.

Thanks to the essayists and poets in this book. I have learned more from reading your drafts and talking with you than I ever dreamed. And I had pretty big expectations. It was a privilege to use your work in this collection, and I think of you and your families often. I was humbled by the stories, the skill with which they were presented, and the grace with which you accepted editorial suggestions, and the tenacity with which some of you argued with me! I am happy to have made contacts with folks whose work didn't make it into this volume. Thanks to you, too.

Thanks to author and poet Marly Youmans, who took time out of her busy writing and family life to judge a poetry contest and spend a lot of time on the phone with me talking about the business and art of books, about fatherhood, and about disability. (And for her consistently overly kind statements about me on Facebook and in her blog.)

Thanks to Beth Gallob, who took time out of her busy schedule and her own life challenges to help me through final editing of the essays and for doing this "on spec." (Readers, please encourage your friends to buy this book so I can pay her!) My relationship with Beth is a testament to keeping in touch with amazing folks you have worked with before.

Thanks to my immediate and extended family for your financial and emotional support as I sort of stopped being "marketing and product manager and entrepreneur dude" and became "writer dude" for a long while. And with you (and I) wondering how exactly how I was going to pay for the mortgage and groceries.

And a special thanks, hugs, and warm brownies to my darling M.A.T., who through her support reminded me that there is indeed still room in my life for love.

To purchase bulk print copies of this collection

- or -

To purchase a site license of an electronic version of this book for your educational, medical, government, NGO, or non-profit organization, please contact gdietz@garydietz.com with "site license" contained in the subject of the email.

To query about contributions of an essay or poem for a future collection, visit http://www.dadsofdisability.com

To receive bonus essays or MP3 files that I may create from time-to-time, drop me a line: gdietz@garydietz.com

Project Website and Blog:
http://www.dadsofdisability.com

On social media

 Like us at
www.facebook.com/dadsofdisability

 Twitter @garymdietz
#dadsofdis

Made in the USA
Charleston, SC
15 March 2014